CHAPTER 1: INTRODUCTION TO PODCASTING

Imagine having your own radio show, but with a global audience. Imagine sharing your voice and your message with the world, and changing the way we consume and create content. Imagine joining the millions of people who are creating and enjoying podcasts every day. This is the power and potential of podcasting, a medium that is native to the Internet and has been evolving for more than two decades. Podcasting is a form of audio content creation that covers a wide range of topics, genres, formats, and styles, catering to diverse audiences and interests. Whether you want to learn something new, be entertained, get inspired, or join a community, there is a podcast for you.

But podcasts are not only for listeners. They are also for creators. Anyone with a microphone, a computer, and an internet connection can start their own podcast and share their voice, stories, opinions, or expertise with the world. Podcasting is a low-cost, high-reach, and creative way to produce and distribute audio content, without being constrained by traditional media gatekeepers or regulations. Some of the most successful podcasters today started from scratch, with no prior experience or formal training, and built loyal fan bases and lucrative businesses. In fact, Twitter, one of the most influential social media platforms today, was born from a failed podcasting platform called Odeo.

Podcasting is not only a medium, but a movement. And you can be a part of it. In this book, you will learn how to podcast like a pro in 2024. You will discover the essential steps and best practices for creating and launching your own podcast, from planning and producing to distributing and promoting. You will also get tips and insights from some of the top podcasters in the industry, who will share their secrets and stories of podcasting success. Whether you are a beginner or an experienced podcaster, this book will help you take your podcast to the next level. If you want to learn how to podcast like a pro in 2024 and join the millions of people who are creating and enjoying podcasts every day, then this book is for you. Don't wait any longer, get your copy today and start your podcasting journey!

According to recent statistics there were over 100 million monthly podcast listeners in the US in 2023, up from 68 million in 2019. Podcasts cover a wide range of topics, genres, formats, and styles, catering to diverse audiences and interests. Whether you want to learn something new, be entertained, get inspired, or join a community, there is a podcast for you.

But podcasts are not only for listeners. They are also for creators. Anyone with a microphone, a computer, and an internet connection can start their own podcast and share their voice, stories, opinions, or expertise with the world. Podcasting is a powerful and accessible medium that allows you to express yourself creatively, connect with your audience, and even generate income.

In this book, you will learn how to podcast like a pro in 2024. You will discover the essential steps and best practices for creating and launching your own podcast, from planning and producing to distributing and promoting. Whether you are a beginner or an experienced podcaster, this book will help you take your podcast to the next level.

Podcasting is a rewarding and fulfilling medium, but it also comes with its own set of challenges and frustrations. Many aspiring podcasters struggle with technical issues, content creation, monetization, and motivation. These are some of the common problems that podcasters face:

Challenges in Podcasting

Podcasting, while a rewarding endeavor, comes with its unique set of challenges that many aspiring podcasters encounter. Recognizing and addressing these hurdles early on can significantly contribute to your podcasting success. Here are some common challenges:

1. **Technical Hurdles:**
   - Recording, editing, and uploading episodes can be daunting, especially for beginners. Challenges may include platform and quality issues, navigating various file formats, choosing suitable hosting platforms, and managing RSS feeds.

2. **Content Creation Struggles:**
   - Consistently producing fresh and engaging content is a common hurdle. Podcasters might encounter difficulties in generating ideas, risk repeating topics, or lose focus on their niche and audience.

3. **Monetization Dilemmas:**
   - Generating income from a podcast, particularly without a substantial audience, can be challenging. Finding sponsors, advertisers, or donors willing to support your podcast can be an uphill battle, especially in a competitive landscape.

4. **Motivational Challenges:**
   - Staying motivated and consistent in podcasting can be tough, especially when immediate results are not visible. Feelings

of discouragement, being overwhelmed, or experiencing burnout are common.

These are some of the challenges that this book will help you overcome. In the upcoming chapters, we'll delve into how to turn what look like obstacles into what they really are - opportunities, providing actionable strategies and insights to help you navigate and overcome each bump in the road to becoming a successful podcaster. Whether you're a novice or an experienced podcaster, understanding and conquering these challenges is vital to ensuring a fulfilling and sustainable podcasting journey.

In this book, you will learn how to podcast like a pro in 2024. You will discover the essential steps and best practices for creating and launching your own podcast, from planning and producing to distributing and promoting.

Here are some of the specific strategies and techniques that you will learn in this book:

- How to choose the right equipment and software for your podcast, and how to set up your recording studio and workflow.

- How to research your target audience and niche, and how to create a content calendar and outline for your episodes.

- How to record, edit, and produce high-quality audio, and how to add music, sound effects, and transitions to your podcast.

- How to upload, host, and distribute your podcast to various platforms, and how to create and manage your RSS feed and website.

- How to market and promote your podcast to attract and retain listeners, and how to use social media, email, and SEO to grow your audience.

- How to monetize your podcast and generate income from various sources, such as sponsors, advertisers, donors, affiliates, and merchandise.

- How to stay motivated and consistent with your podcast, and how to overcome challenges and setbacks along the way.
- How to measure and improve your podcast performance, and how to use analytics, feedback, and reviews to optimize your podcast.

By applying these strategies and techniques to your own podcasting projects, you will be able to create a successful and sustainable podcast that will serve your purpose and reach your goals. You will also be able to enjoy the benefits of podcasting, such as expressing yourself creatively, connecting with your audience, and generating income.

In this chapter, we will cover the following topics:
- The evolution and current state of podcasting
- Exploring the popularity and potential of podcasts in 2024
- Success stories of notable podcasters

The evolution and current state of podcasting
Podcasting, as a medium, is native to the Internet. It's the result of various collaborations between people from all over the world and is still evolving to this day. The term "podcast" was coined by Ben Hammersley in 2004, as a portmanteau of "iPod" and "broadcast". However, the concept of delivering audio content over the web dates back to the late 1990s, when software developers created programs that allowed users to download and sync audio files to portable devices.

The early pioneers of podcasting included Adam Curry, a former MTV VJ who created a show called Daily Source Code, and Dave Winer, a software developer who created Really Simple Syndication (RSS) feeds that enabled automatic downloads of audio files. They were joined by other enthusiasts who experimented with different formats, topics, and styles of podcasting, such as comedy, music, news, education, and more.

The popularity of podcasting grew steadily over the years, as more people discovered the medium and its benefits. Podcasts offered listeners a convenient, personalized, and engaging way to consume audio content, without being limited by time, location, or device. Podcasts also offered creators a low-cost, high-reach, and creative way to produce and distribute audio content, without being constrained by traditional media gatekeepers or regulations.

The podcasting industry reached several milestones in the past decade, such as:
- The launch of Apple Podcasts supported by ITunes in 2005, which became the dominant platform for podcast discovery and consumption.
- The emergence of podcast networks, such as NPR, Gimlet, Wondery, and iHeartMedia, which produced and distributed high-quality, original, and diverse podcasts.
- The rise of podcast advertising, which generated over $1 billion in revenue in 2021, and is projected to grow to $4 billion by 2024.
- The expansion of podcast genres, such as true crime, fiction, sports, and more, which attracted new and niche audiences.
- The entry of new players, such as Spotify, Amazon, and Google, which invested in podcast content, technology, and distribution.
- The emergence of podcast stars, such as Joe Rogan, Conan O'Brien, Emma Chamberlain, and more, who leveraged their existing fame or built their own brand through podcasting.

As of 2023, there were over 4 million podcasts registered around the world, covering almost every topic imaginable. Podcasting has become a mainstream and influential medium, that has changed the way people listen, learn, and communicate.

Exploring the popularity and potential of podcasts in 2024

Podcasting is not only popular, but also has a lot of potential for growth and innovation in 2024 and beyond. According to various sources, podcasting has the following characteristics and trends:

- Podcasting has a large and loyal audience. In 2023, 42% of

Americans ages 12 and older had listened to a podcast in the past month, and 31% had listened to a podcast in the past week. Podcast listeners tend to be younger, more educated, and more affluent than the general population. Podcast listeners also tend to consume more podcasts than other types of media, with an average of 8 podcasts per week. Podcast listeners are also highly engaged and trusting of podcast hosts and advertisers.

- Podcasting has a global and diverse reach. Podcasting is not only popular in the US, but also in other countries, such as China, India, Brazil, and more. Podcasting also offers opportunities for cross-cultural and cross-lingual communication and collaboration.

- Podcasting has a lot of room for innovation and experimentation. Podcasting is still a relatively young and evolving medium, that offers a lot of possibilities for creativity and improvement. Podcasting can incorporate new technologies, such as artificial intelligence, voice assistants, interactive audio, and more. Podcasting can also explore new formats, genres, styles, and topics, such as live podcasts, immersive podcasts, hybrid podcasts, and more. Podcasting can also create new business models, such as subscription, donation, sponsorship, and more.

Success stories of notable podcasters

Podcasting has produced many success stories of notable podcasters, who have achieved fame, fortune, and impact through their podcasts. Here are some examples of podcasters who have inspired millions of listeners and creators:

- **John Lee Dumas**: Entrepreneur on Fire. John Lee Dumas is the owner and host of Entrepreneur on Fire, a top-ranked business podcast that interviews the most inspiring entrepreneurs in the world. He started his podcast in 2012, after quitting his job and finding his passion for podcasting. He has since interviewed over 3000 entrepreneurs, such as Tony Robbins, Gary Vaynerchuk, Tim Ferriss, and more. He has also built a multimillion-dollar podcasting empire, with four flagship products: The Fire Nation, Podcasters' Paradise, WebinarOnFire, and The Fire Path.

- **Jaime Tardy:** Eventual Millionaire. Jaime Tardy is the owner and host of Eventual Millionaire, a podcast and a blog that features interviews with millionaires and advice on how to become one. She started her podcast in 2010, after paying off her $70,000 debt and quitting her job. She decided to pursue her childhood dream of becoming a millionaire and learn from those who had already done it. She has since interviewed over 500 millionaires, such as Seth Godin, Barbara Corcoran, Guy Kawasaki, and more. She has also written a bestselling book and become a sought-after business coach and speaker.

- **Tim Ferriss**: The Tim Ferriss Show. Tim Ferriss is the owner and host of The Tim Ferriss Show, a podcast that explores the habits, routines, and tactics of world-class performers, from various fields and disciplines. He started his podcast in 2014, after being a successful author, entrepreneur, and investor. He wanted to share his curiosity and learn from the best in the world, and also have fun and experiment with podcasting. He has since interviewed over 500 guests, such as Arnold Schwarzenegger, LeBron James, Oprah Winfrey, and more. He has also won multiple awards and become one of the most influential podcasters in the world.

- **Pat Flynn**: Smart Passive Income. Pat Flynn is the owner and host of Smart Passive Income, a podcast and a blog that teaches people how to create and grow online businesses that generate passive income. He started his podcast in 2010, after being laid off from his architecture job and discovering the power of online entrepreneurship. He wanted to share his journey and lessons learned, and also help others achieve their financial and lifestyle goals. He has since created over 500 episodes, covering topics such as blogging, podcasting, affiliate marketing, and more. He has also launched several successful online courses, books, and software, and become a leader in the online business space.

- **Amy Porterfield**: Online Marketing Made Easy. Amy Porterfield is the owner and host of Online Marketing Made Easy, a podcast that helps entrepreneurs build profitable online businesses using digital marketing strategies. She started her podcast in 2013, after working as a corporate marketing trainer and a social media consultant. She wanted to share her expertise and experience, and also connect with her audience and potential customers. She has since produced over 400 episodes, covering topics such as email marketing, webinars, online courses, and more. She has also created several successful online programs, such as List Builders Society, Digital Course Academy, and Momentum Membership.

You have just learned about the power and potential of podcasting, a medium that allows you to share your voice and your message with the world, and to enjoy the benefits of creativity, connection, and income. You have also learned about the challenges and frustrations that many podcasters face, and how this book will help you overcome them. You have also learned about the specific strategies and techniques that this book will teach you, and how they will help you create a successful and sustainable podcast.

Now, the only thing left to do is to take action. If you want to learn how to podcast like a pro in 2024 and join the millions of people who are creating and enjoying podcasts every day, then this book is for you. Don't wait any longer, get your copy today and start your podcasting journey! This is your chance to turn your passion into a podcast, and your podcast into a purpose. Click the button below and get instant access to the book. **Podcast like a pro in 2024!**

CHAPTER 2: CHOOSING YOUR NICHE AND FORMAT

One of the most important decisions you will make as a podcaster is choosing your niche and format. Your niche is the specific topic or theme of your podcast, and your format is the way you present your content. Your niche and format will determine the value, style, and audience of your podcast. In this chapter, we will cover the following topics:

- Identifying your passion and expertise
- Analyzing market trends and audience demand
- Selecting the right podcast format for your content

Identifying your passion and expertise

The first step in choosing your niche and format is identifying your passion and expertise. You should choose a niche and format that you are genuinely interested in and knowledgeable about. This will help you create engaging and valuable content for your listeners, and also keep you motivated and inspired as a podcaster.

To identify your passion and expertise, you can ask yourself the following questions:

- What are you passionate about? What topics or themes do you enjoy learning, talking, or writing about? What are your hobbies, interests, or goals?

- What are you good at? What skills or knowledge do you have that you can share with others? What are your strengths, talents, or experiences?

- What are you curious about? What topics or themes do you want to learn more about or explore? What are your questions, challenges, or problems?

You can also brainstorm a list of possible niches and formats based on your answers, and use a mind map, a spreadsheet, or a notebook to organize your ideas. You can also use online tools, such as AnswerThePublic, BuzzSumo, or Google Trends, to find out what people are searching for, talking about, or interested in, related to your niches and formats.

Analyzing market trends and audience demand

The second step in choosing your niche and format is analyzing market trends and audience demand. You should choose a niche and format that has a clear and defined target audience and market. You need to know who your ideal listeners are, what their needs, wants, problems, and goals are, and how you can help them, entertain them, or educate them. You should also choose a niche and format that has sufficient and sustainable demand and potential for growth, and that is not too saturated or competitive.

To analyze market trends and audience demand, you can use the following methods and tools:

- **Keyword research**. You can use online tools, such as Keyword Planner, Podcast Analytics, or iTunes Charts, to find out the popularity, demand, and competition of your niches and formats. You can look for keywords or phrases that have high search volume, low competition, and high relevance to your niches and formats.

- **Audience research**. You can use online platforms, such as social media, forums, blogs, or surveys, to ask questions, conduct polls, or join discussions, related to your niches and formats. You can look for feedback, opinions, preferences, pain points, or suggestions from your potential listeners.

- **Competitor research.** You can use online tools, such as Chartable, Podchaser, or Podnews, to find out who your competitors are, what they are doing, and how they are performing. You can look for their strengths, weaknesses, opportunities, or threats, and learn from their successes or mistakes.

Selecting the right podcast format for your content

The third step in choosing your niche and format is selecting the right podcast format for your content. Your podcast format is the way you present your content, such as solo, interview, panel, or storytelling. Your podcast format will affect the tone, style, and length of your podcast, and also the resources, equipment, and skills you will need.

To select the right podcast format for your content, you can consider the following factors:

- **Your content type and purpose**. You should choose a podcast format that matches the type and purpose of your content. For example, if your content is educational or informative, you might choose a solo or interview format, where you can share your knowledge or expertise, or learn from an expert. If your content is entertaining or inspirational, you might choose a panel or storytelling format, where you can create a lively or immersive experience for your listeners.

- **Your personal preference and style**. You should choose a podcast format that suits your personal preference and style. For example, if you are comfortable and confident speaking alone, you might choose a solo format, where you can have full control and flexibility over your content. If you enjoy interacting and collaborating with others, you might choose a co-hosted or panel format, where you can have a conversation and exchange ideas with your partners or guests.

- **Your audience expectation and feedback.** You should choose a podcast format that meets your audience expectations and feedback. For example, if your audience expects or prefers a certain format, you might choose that format, or adapt it to your niche and content. If your audience gives you positive or negative feedback on your format, you might keep or change it, or improve it based on their suggestions.

The Crucial Role of Flexibility in Your Podcasting Journey

While selecting a niche and format lays the foundation for your podcast, embracing flexibility is the key to sustained success. In the dynamic landscape of podcasting, being open to adaptation is as crucial as making your initial choices.

Why Flexibility Matters:

1. **Evolving Interests:** Your passion and interests may evolve over time. Allowing room for these changes ensures your content remains authentic and engaging.

2. **Listener Feedback:** Pay attention to your audience's feedback. Flexibility enables you to respond to what your listeners enjoy and tailor your content accordingly.

3. **Industry Trends:** Podcasting trends and listener preferences may shift. Flexibility allows you to incorporate new formats or topics that resonate with the ever-changing podcast audience.

How to Embrace Flexibility:

1. **Regularly Assess Your Content:** Take stock of your episodes, analyzing what works well and what can be improved. This ongoing assessment sets the stage for positive adjustments.

2. **Stay Informed:** Keep yourself updated on industry trends, emerging topics, and new formats. Embracing change and staying informed positions your podcast as relevant and current.

3. **Engage with Your Community:** Foster a community

around your podcast. Regularly interact with your audience through social media, surveys, or live sessions. This engagement provides valuable insights into their preferences.

SEO-Friendly Tip: Emphasize adaptability and flexibility in your podcasting journey. Search engines appreciate dynamic content that responds to user needs, making your podcast more discoverable.

Remember, flexibility doesn't mean abandoning your niche; it means enhancing it. By staying flexible, you ensure that your podcast grows with you and continues to captivate your audience.

In this section, we will compare the pros and cons of some of the most popular podcast formats and give you some examples of successful podcasts that use them.

- **Solo**: This is when you host your podcast by yourself and talk about your topic or niche. Some of the pros of this format are that you have full control and flexibility over your content, you can establish your credibility and authority as an expert, and you can save time and money on finding and scheduling guests or co-hosts. Some of the cons of this format are that you might feel lonely or bored speaking alone, you might run out of ideas or topics to talk about, and you might have a hard time engaging or retaining your listeners. Some examples of solo podcasts are The Tim Ferriss Show, Smart Passive Income, and Online Marketing Made Easy.

- **Interview**: This is when you host your podcast with one or more guests and ask them questions about your topic or niche. Some of the pros of this format are that you can learn from and network with experts or influencers in your niche, you can provide valuable and diverse content for your listeners, and you can attract and grow your audience by leveraging your guests' fan base. Some of the cons of this format are that you might have a hard time finding and scheduling suitable and reliable guests, you might have a hard time preparing and conducting effective and interesting interviews, and you might have a hard time standing out from other interview podcasts. Some examples of interview podcasts are Entrepreneur on Fire, Eventual Millionaire, and The Joe Rogan Experience.

- **Panel**: This is when you host your podcast with two or more co-hosts or guests and have a discussion or debate about your topic or niche. Some of the pros of this format are that you can create lively and dynamic content with multiple perspectives and opinions, you can share the workload and responsibility with your co-hosts or guests, and you can appeal to a wider and more diverse audience. Some of the cons of this format are that you might have a hard time finding and coordinating with compatible and cooperative co-hosts or guests, you might have a hard time managing and moderating the discussion and avoiding conflicts or arguments, and you might have a hard time ensuring the audio quality and editing the podcast. Some examples of panel podcasts are The View, The Bugle, and The Guilty Feminist.

- **Storytelling**: This is when you host your podcast with a narrative structure and elements and tell a story about your topic or niche. Some of the pros of this format are that you can create immersive and captivating content with a narrative structure and elements, you can showcase your creativity and originality as a storyteller, and you can build a loyal and engaged audience who will follow your story. Some of the cons of this format are that you might have a hard time planning and writing a compelling and coherent story, you might have a hard time producing and performing a high-quality and professional audio drama, and you might have a hard time monetizing and sustaining your podcast. Some examples of storytelling podcasts are Serial, Welcome to Night Vale, and The Adventure Zone.

By choosing your niche and format, you will have a clear vision and strategy for your podcast, and you will be able to create and deliver content that is relevant, valuable, and engaging for your listeners. You will also be able to stand out from the crowd and attract and retain your ideal audience and market.

CHAPTER 3: PLANNING YOUR PODCAST

After you have chosen your niche and format for your podcast, the next step is to plan your podcast in detail. Planning your podcast will help you create consistent, engaging, and valuable content for your listeners, and also save you time and effort in the long run. In this chapter, we will cover the following topics:

- Crafting a compelling podcast concept
- Structuring episodes for engagement
- Creating an editorial calendar

Crafting a compelling podcast concept

Your podcast concept is the core idea or message of your podcast. It is what makes your podcast unique and appealing to your target audience. Your podcast concept should answer the following questions:

- What is your podcast about?
- Who is your podcast for?
- Why should they listen to your podcast?
- How will your podcast help, entertain, or educate them?

To craft a compelling podcast concept, you can use the following steps:

- Write down your podcast's main topic or theme in one sentence. For example, "My podcast is about podcasting."
- Identify your podcast's subtopics or categories that

relate to your main topic or theme. For example, "My podcast covers podcast planning, production, distribution, and promotion."

· Define your podcast's unique selling proposition (USP) or value proposition. This is what sets your podcast apart from other podcasts in your niche or format. For example, "My podcast teaches you how to podcast like a pro in 2024, with tips and insights from top podcasters in the industry."

· Write down your podcast's mission statement or vision statement. This is what your podcast aims to achieve or accomplish for your listeners. For example, "My podcast's mission is to help aspiring and experienced podcasters create and launch their own podcasts and take them to the next level."

Structuring episodes for engagement

Your podcast episodes are the individual pieces of content that make up your podcast. Each episode should have a clear and specific topic, goal, and structure. Your podcast episode structure is the way you organize and present your content, such as the introduction, the main content, and the outro. Your podcast episode structure will affect the flow, pace, and length of your episode, and also the listener's experience and satisfaction.

To structure your episodes for engagement, you can use the following steps:

· Write down your episode's main topic or theme in one sentence. For example, "This episode is about how to plan your podcast with scripts and templates."

· Write down your episode's main goal or purpose in one sentence. For example, "This episode's goal is to teach you how to plan your podcast with scripts and templates, and why it's important to do so."

· Write down your episode's main points or arguments that support your topic and goal. For example, "This episode's main points are: how to write a podcast script, how to use podcast show templates, how to structure and script your podcast segments, and how to use podcast interview formats."

- Write down your episode's intro script. This is the first part of your episode that introduces your podcast, your topic, your goal, and your main points. Your intro script should be short, catchy, and informative. For example, "Welcome to Podcast Like a Pro, the podcast that teaches you how to podcast like a pro in 2024. I'm your host, John Smith, and in this episode, we're going to talk about how to plan your podcast with scripts and templates. Planning your podcast is one of the most important steps in creating a successful podcast, and in this episode, I'll show you how to do it in a simple and effective way. We'll cover how to write a podcast script, how to use podcast show templates, how to structure and script your podcast segments, and how to use podcast interview formats. By the end of this episode, you'll be able to plan your podcast like a pro and create engaging and valuable content for your listeners. So, let's get started."

- Write down your episode's main content script. This is the main part of your episode that delivers your content, your main points, and your arguments. Your main content script should be clear, concise, and compelling. You can use different formats, such as solo, interview, panel, or storytelling, depending on your podcast format and episode topic. You can also use different elements, such as stories, examples, facts, statistics, quotes, or testimonials, to support your points and arguments. For example, "The first thing you need to do when planning your podcast is to write a podcast script. A podcast script is a document that outlines the content and structure of your episode. It helps you organize your thoughts, stay on topic, and avoid rambling or repeating yourself. A podcast script also helps you improve your delivery, your tone, and your pace, and make your episode more professional and polished. There are different types of podcast scripts, such as full scripts, bullet point scripts, or outline scripts, depending on how much detail you want to include. You can also use different tools, such as Google Docs, Evernote, or Trello, to write and store your podcast scripts. To write a good podcast script, you should follow these steps: ... "

. Write down your episode's outro script. This is the last part of your episode that wraps up your content, your main points, and your arguments. Your outro script should be brief, memorable, and actionable. You can also use your outro script to thank your listeners, invite feedback, promote your podcast, or tease your next episode. For example, "That's it for this episode of Podcast Like a Pro. I hope you learned something new and useful about how to plan your podcast with scripts and templates. Remember, planning your podcast is one of the most important steps in creating a successful podcast, and it will help you create consistent, engaging, and valuable content for your listeners. If you enjoyed this episode, please leave a review on iTunes, Spotify, or wherever you listen to podcasts. It really helps us grow and reach more people like you. You can also send me your questions, comments, or suggestions at podcastlikeapro@gmail.com, or follow me on Twitter @podcastlikeapro. In the next episode, we'll talk about how to produce your podcast with the right equipment and setup. You don't want to miss it, so make sure you subscribe to Podcast Like a Pro and stay tuned. Until then, happy podcasting!"

Creating an editorial calendar

Your podcast editorial calendar is a tool that helps you plan, schedule, and manage your podcast content. It helps you keep track of your episode topics, guests, deadlines, and publishing dates. It also helps you align your podcast content with your marketing goals, your audience's needs, and your industry's trends. Your podcast editorial calendar can be a simple spreadsheet, a calendar app, or a project management tool, depending on your preference and needs.

To create an editorial calendar for your podcast, you can use the following steps:

- Write down your podcast's frequency and duration. How often and how long do you want to publish your podcast episodes? For example, "I want to publish my podcast episodes weekly, and each episode should be around 30 minutes long."

- Write down your podcast's main themes or categories. What are the main topics or themes that you want to cover in your podcast? For example, "My podcast's main themes are podcast planning, production, distribution, and promotion."

- Write down your podcast's subtopics or ideas. What are the specific subtopics or ideas that you want to cover in each theme or category? For example, "My podcast's subtopics for podcast planning are: how to write a podcast script, how to use podcast show templates, how to structure and script your podcast segments, and how to use podcast interview formats."

- Write down your podcast's guests or sources. Who are the potential guests or sources that you want to feature or consult in your podcast episodes? For example, "My podcast's guests for podcast planning are: Tim Ferriss, Oprah Winfrey, and Joe Rogan."

- Write down your podcast's deadlines and publishing dates. When do you want to record, edit, and publish your podcast episodes? For example, "My podcast's deadlines and publishing dates for podcast planning are: record by Monday, edit by Wednesday, publish by Friday."

- Write down your podcast's promotion and evaluation methods. How do you want to promote and evaluate your podcast episodes? For example, "My podcast's promotion and evaluation methods for podcast planning are: share on social media, email newsletter, and website, and measure downloads, reviews, and feedback."

You can use these steps to create an editorial calendar for your podcast and update it regularly as you go along. You can also use some of the web search results I found for you to learn more about how to create an editorial calendar for your podcast. How to Plan Your Podcast with Scripts and Templates is a helpful article that shares the author's personal experience and advice on planning a podcast. How to Plan a Podcast: Structure Your Episodes is another useful article that explains how to structure your episodes for engagement. How to Start a Podcast: Launch to Growth Made Simple 2024 is a comprehensive guide that covers everything you need to know about starting a podcast, including how to create an editorial calendar.

CHAPTER 4: RECORDING AND EQUIPMENT

After you have planned your podcast concept, niche, format, and structure, the next step is to record your podcast with the right equipment and software. Recording your podcast will require you to choose the best microphone, headphones, and recording space for your podcast, as well as the best recording software for your needs. In this chapter, we will cover the following topics:

- Choosing the right microphone, headphones, and recording space
- Overview of recording software
- Tips for high-quality audio production

Choosing the right microphone, headphones, and recording space

Your microphone, headphones, and recording space are the three main factors that affect the quality of your podcast audio. You should choose the best equipment and environment for your podcast, depending on your budget, your podcast format, and your personal preference.

Microphone

Your microphone is the device that captures your voice and converts it into an electrical signal. There are different types of microphones, such as dynamic, condenser, USB, or XLR, depending on how they work, how they connect to your computer, and how they sound. You should choose a microphone that suits your podcast format, your voice, and your recording space.

Dynamic microphones are the most common and affordable type of microphones for podcasting. They are durable, versatile, and easy to use. They are also good at rejecting background noise and handling loud sounds. However, they may not capture the full range and detail of your voice, and they may require a preamp or an audio interface to boost their signal.

Condenser microphones are more sensitive and expensive than dynamic microphones. They are good at capturing the nuances and clarity of your voice, and they can produce a rich and warm sound. However, they may also pick up more background noise and room echo, and they may require phantom power or a battery to work.

USB microphones are microphones that connect directly to your computer via a USB port. They are convenient, portable, and easy to set up. They are also good for solo podcasters or beginners who don't want to deal with complicated audio equipment. However, they may not offer the same sound quality and flexibility as other types of microphones, and they may not work well with multiple microphones or guests.

XLR microphones are microphones that connect to your computer via an XLR cable and an audio interface or a mixer. They are professional, reliable, and customizable. They are also good for podcasters who want more control and options over their sound, and who want to record with multiple microphones or guests. However, they may be more expensive, complex, and bulky than other types of microphones, and they may require more technical skills and knowledge to use.

Some of the best microphones for podcasting are:

- **Shure SM58**: A classic dynamic microphone that is durable, versatile, and affordable. It is good for podcasters who want a simple and reliable microphone that can handle any situation. It has a cardioid polar pattern that rejects background noise and a built-in pop filter that reduces plosives. It has an XLR connection and requires an audio interface or a mixer to work. Shure SM58

- **Blue Yeti**: A popular USB microphone that is convenient, portable, and easy to use. It is good for podcasters who want a plug-and-play microphone that can record in different modes. It has a tri-capsule array that allows you to switch between four polar patterns: cardioid, bidirectional, omnidirectional, and stereo. It also has a headphone jack, a mute button, and gain control. Blue Yeti

- **Rode PodMic**: A dynamic microphone that is designed specifically for podcasting. It is good for podcasters who want a professional and stylish microphone that can produce a crisp and clear sound. It has a cardioid polar pattern that rejects background noise and a built-in pop filter that reduces plosives. It has an XLR connection and requires an audio interface or a mixer to work. Rode PodMic

- **Audio-Technica AT2020**: A condenser microphone that is sensitive and affordable. It is good for podcasters who want a microphone that can capture the detail and clarity of their voice. It has a cardioid polar pattern that reduces background noise and a low-mass diaphragm that provides a wide frequency response. It has an XLR connection and requires phantom power or a battery to work. Audio-Technica AT2020

Headphones

Your headphones are the device that allows you to listen to your voice and your audio while recording and editing your podcast. There are different types of headphones, such as earbuds, on-ear, or over-ear, depending on how they fit on your ears, how they isolate sound, and how they sound. You should choose headphones that are comfortable, durable, and accurate for your podcast.

Earbuds are headphones that fit inside your ear canal. They are lightweight, compact, and discreet. They are also good for podcasters who want to record on the go, or who don't want to mess up their hair. However, they may not offer the best sound quality and isolation, and they may cause ear fatigue or irritation.

On-ear headphones are headphones that rest on your ears. They are comfortable, portable, and affordable. They are also good for podcasters who want to record in a quiet environment, or who want to hear some ambient sound. However, they may not offer the best sound quality and isolation, and they may leak sound or cause ear pressure.

Over-ear headphones are headphones that cover your ears. They are bulky, expensive, and immersive. They are also good for podcasters who want to record in a noisy environment, or who want to hear the best sound quality and isolation. However, they may be too hot, heavy, or tight for some people, and they may block out too much sound or cause ear sweating.

Some of the best headphones for podcasting are:

- **Sony MDR7506:** A classic over-ear headphone that is professional, reliable, and affordable. It is good for podcasters who want headphones that can deliver a clear and accurate sound. It has a closed-back design that isolates sound and a 40mm driver that provides a wide frequency response. It also has a foldable design, a coiled cable, and a 3.5mm plug with a 6.3mm adapter. Sony MDR7506

- **Sennheiser HD 280 Pro**: An over-ear headphone that is durable, comfortable, and versatile. It is good for podcasters who want headphones that can handle a variety of audio sources and environments. It has a closed-back design that isolates sound and a 32mm driver that provides a balanced sound. It also has a collapsible design, a coiled cable, and a 3.5mm plug with a 6.3mm adapter. [Sennheiser HD 280 Pro]

- **Audio-Technica ATH-M50x:** An over-ear headphone that is popular, stylish, and high-quality. It is good for podcasters who want headphones that can produce a crisp and detailed sound. It has a closed-back design that isolates sound and a 45mm driver that provides a wide frequency response. It also has a swivel design, a detachable cable, and a 3.5mm plug with a 6.3mm adapter. [Audio-Technica ATH-M50x]

- **Bose QuietComfort 20**: An earbud headphone that is lightweight, compact, and noise canceling. It is good for podcasters who want headphones that can reduce background noise and enhance their voice. It has an in-ear design that isolates sound and a dual-microphone system that provides a clear sound. It also has a rechargeable battery, a control module, and a 3.5mm plug. [Bose QuietComfort 20]

Recording space

Your recording space is the environment where you record your podcast. It affects the quality of your podcast audio by adding or reducing noise, echo, or reverb. You should choose a recording space that is quiet, dry, and comfortable for your podcast.

Quiet means that your recording space has minimal or no external noise, such as traffic, people, or animals. You can choose a recording space that is away from sources of noise, such as windows, doors, or vents. You can also use noise-canceling headphones, a noise gate, or noise reduction software to reduce noise.

Dry means that your recording space has minimal or no internal echo or reverb, which are the reflections of sound waves from the walls, floor, or ceiling. You can choose a recording space that has soft or irregular surfaces, such as carpets, curtains, or furniture.

You can also use acoustic foam, blankets, or pillows to absorb echo or reverb.

Comfortable means that your recording space has optimal temperature, humidity, and lighting for your podcast. You can choose a recording space that has a thermostat, a humidifier, or a lamp to adjust the conditions. You can also use a water bottle, a fan, or a heater to stay hydrated, cool, or warm.

Sure, I'll try to continue the draft for you based on your outline. Here's what I came up with:

Overview of recording software

Your recording software is the program that allows you to record, edit, and export your podcast audio. There are different types of recording software, such as free, paid, online, or offline, depending on their features, functions, and prices. You should choose recording software that meets your needs, your budget, and your skill level.

Free recording software are programs that you can download and use for free, without any limitations or restrictions. They are good for podcasters who want to save money, or who want to try out podcasting before investing in more advanced software. However, they may not offer the best sound quality, user interface, or customer support, and they may have bugs or compatibility issues.

Paid recording software are programs that you have to pay for, either as a one-time purchase or a subscription. They are good for podcasters who want to get the best sound quality, features, and functions, and who want to have access to updates, tutorials, and customer support. However, they may be too expensive, complex, or unnecessary for some podcasters, and they may require more storage space or processing power.

Online recording software are programs that you can access and use via a web browser, without downloading or installing anything. They are good for podcasters who want to record on the go, or who want to collaborate with other podcasters remotely.

However, they may not offer the same sound quality, features, or functions as offline software, and they may require a stable internet connection and a cloud storage account.

Offline recording software are programs that you have to download and install on your computer, and that you can use without an internet connection. They are good for podcasters who want to have more control and options over their recording, editing, and exporting process, and who want to work offline. However, they may be more difficult to set up, update, or troubleshoot, and they may not work well with other devices or platforms.

Some of the best recording software for podcasting are:

- **Audacity**: A free, open-source, and cross-platform recording software that is easy to use and versatile. It is good for podcasters who want simple and reliable software that can record, edit, and export audio in various formats. It also has a range of effects, filters, and plugins that can enhance your audio quality and creativity. Audacity

- **GarageBand**: A free, Apple-only, and user-friendly recording software that is designed for music production. It is good for podcasters who want software that can record, edit, and export audio with high quality and style. It also has a variety of instruments, loops, and sounds that can add music and flair to your podcast. GarageBand

- **Adobe Audition**: A paid, professional, and powerful recording software that is part of the Adobe Creative Cloud suite. It is good for podcasters who want software that can record, edit, and export audio with the best quality and features. It also has a multitrack editor, a spectral editor, and a noise reduction tool that can handle complex and advanced audio editing tasks. Adobe Audition

- **Zencastr**: An online, subscription-based, and collaborative recording software that is designed for podcasting. It is good for podcasters who want software that can record, edit, and export audio with ease and convenience. It also has a cloud storage integration, a soundboard, and a post-production service that can simplify and streamline your podcasting workflow. Zencastr

Tips for high-quality audio production

Your audio production is the process of recording, editing, and exporting your podcast audio. It affects the quality of your podcast audio by enhancing or reducing the sound, clarity, and consistency of your voice and content. You should follow some tips and best practices for high-quality audio production for your podcast.

- Test your equipment and software before recording. Make sure your microphone, headphones, and recording software are working properly and are compatible with each other. Adjust the settings and levels to suit your voice and environment. Do a test recording and listen to it to check the sound quality and identify any issues or problems.

- Record in a quiet, dry, and comfortable space. Choose a recording space that has minimal or no external noise, echo, or reverb, and that has optimal temperature, humidity, and lighting. Use noise-canceling headphones, a noise gate, or noise reduction software to reduce noise. Use acoustic foam, blankets, or pillows to absorb echo or reverb. Use a water bottle, a fan, or a heater to stay hydrated, cool, or warm.

- Speak clearly, confidently, and naturally. Use a good posture, a relaxed tone, and a moderate pace when speaking. Avoid mumbling, stuttering, or whispering. Use a pop filter, a windscreen, or a foam cover to reduce plosives, sibilance, or breath sounds. Use a script, an outline, or a cue card to stay on topic and avoid rambling or repeating yourself.

- Edit your audio carefully and creatively. Use good recording software to edit your audio. Cut out any mistakes, pauses, or filler words. Adjust the volume, pitch, and speed of your audio. Add effects, filters, or plugins to enhance your audio quality and creativity. Add music, sounds, or transitions to add interest and variety to your audio. Use a multitrack editor, a spectral editor, or a noise reduction tool to handle complex and advanced audio editing tasks.

- Export your audio in the right format and quality. Use good recording software to export your audio. Choose the right format, such as MP3, WAV, or AAC, depending on your podcast platform and audience. Choose the right quality, such as bitrate, sample rate, or channels, depending on your audio content and size. Use a metadata editor, a tag editor, or an ID3 editor to add information and details to your audio file.

CHAPTER 5: EDITING AND PRODUCTION

After you have recorded your podcast with the right equipment and software, the next step is to edit and produce your podcast with the right tools and techniques. Editing and producing your podcast will help you enhance the quality, clarity, and consistency of your podcast audio, and also add some flair and personality to your podcast. In this chapter, we will cover the following topics:

- Step-by-step guide to editing podcast episodes
- Adding intros, outros, and music
- Ensuring a professional final product

Step-by-step guide to editing podcast episodes

Editing your podcast episodes is the process of cutting, trimming, and rearranging your audio files to remove any mistakes, pauses, or filler words, and to create a smooth and coherent flow of your content. Editing your podcast episodes will make your podcast sound more professional and polished, and also improve the listening experience and satisfaction for your audience.

To edit your podcast episodes, you can use the following steps:

- Import your audio files into your editing software. You can use any of the recording software we mentioned in the previous chapter, such as Audacity, GarageBand, Adobe Audition, or Zencastr, or you can use a dedicated editing software, such as Hindenburg Journalist, Reaper, or Descript. You can also use an online editing platform, such as Alitu, Podbean, or Podcastle, to edit your podcast episodes without downloading or installing anything.

· Listen to your audio files and mark the parts you want to edit. You can use a pen and paper, a spreadsheet, or a note-taking app to jot down the timestamps and notes of the parts you want to edit, such as ums, ahs, coughs, stutters, or tangents. You can also use the editing software's built-in features, such as labels, markers, or regions, to mark the parts you want to edit.

· Cut out the parts you want to edit. You can use the editing software's tools, such as the selection tool, the razor tool, or the delete key, to highlight and delete the parts you want to edit. You can also use the editing software's shortcuts, such as Ctrl+X, Cmd+X, or Z, to cut out the parts you want to edit faster and easier.

· Rearrange the parts you want to keep. You can use the editing software's tools, such as the move tool, the drag and drop feature, or the copy and paste feature, to move and arrange the parts you want to keep in the order you want. You can also use the editing software's shortcuts, such as Ctrl+V, Cmd+V, or V, to paste the parts you want to keep faster and easier.

· Add transitions between the parts you want to keep. You can use the editing software's tools, such as the fade tool, the crossfade tool, or the envelope tool, to create smooth and seamless transitions between the parts you want to keep. You can also use the editing software's effects, such as the reverb effect, the delay effect, or the echo effect, to create more interesting and creative transitions between the parts you want to keep.

Adding intros, outros, and music

Adding intros, outros, and music to your podcast episodes is the process of inserting pre-recorded or custom-made audio clips to introduce, conclude, and enhance your podcast content. Adding intros, outros, and music to your podcast episodes will help you create a consistent and recognizable brand identity for your podcast, and also add some interest and variety to your podcast.

To add intros, outros, and music to your podcast episodes, you can use the following steps:

- Import your intro, outro, and music files into your editing software. You can use any of the editing software we mentioned in the previous section, or you can use a dedicated music production software, such as Logic Pro, FL Studio, or Ableton Live, to create your own intro, outro, and music files. You can also use an online music platform, such as Epidemic Sound, Artlist, or Soundstripe, to find and download royalty-free music for your podcast.

- Align your intro, outro, and music files with your podcast content. You can use the editing software's tools, such as the move tool, the drag and drop feature, or the snap to grid feature, to align your intro, outro, and music files with your podcast content. You can also use the editing software's shortcuts, such as Ctrl+L, Cmd+L, or L, to align your intro, outro, and music files with your podcast content faster and easier.

- Adjust the volume, pitch, and speed of your intro, outro, and music files. You can use the editing software's tools, such as the volume tool, the pitch tool, or the speed tool, to adjust the volume, pitch, and speed of your intro, outro, and music files to suit your podcast content. You can also use the editing software's effects, such as the compressor effect, the equalizer effect, or the limiter effect, to adjust the volume, pitch, and speed of your intro, outro, and music files to improve their sound quality and consistency.

- Add transitions between your intro, outro, and music files and your podcast content. You can use the editing software's tools, such as the fade tool, the crossfade tool, or the envelope tool, to create smooth and seamless transitions between your intro, outro, and music files and your podcast content. You can also use the editing software's effects, such as the reverb effect, the delay effect, or the echo effect, to create more interesting and creative transitions between your intro, outro, and music files and your podcast content.

Ensuring a professional final product

Ensuring a professional final product for your podcast episodes is the process of applying the final touches and checks to your podcast audio before exporting and publishing it. Ensuring a professional final product for your podcast episodes will help you avoid any errors, glitches, or inconsistencies in your podcast audio, and also optimize it for the best listening experience and satisfaction for your audience.

To ensure a professional final product for your podcast episodes, you can use the following steps:

- Listen to your podcast audio and check for any errors, glitches, or inconsistencies. You can use a pair of headphones, a pair of speakers, or a pair of earbuds to listen to your podcast audio and check for any errors, glitches, or inconsistencies, such as pops, clicks, hisses, hums, or distortions. You can also use the editing software's tools, such as the zoom tool, the waveform tool, or the spectrogram tool, to visualize and identify any errors, glitches, or inconsistencies in your podcast audio.

- Fix any errors, glitches, or inconsistencies in your podcast audio. You can use the editing software's tools, such as the selection tool, the razor tool, or the delete key, to highlight and delete any errors, glitches, or inconsistencies in your podcast audio. You can also use the editing software's effects, such as the noise reduction effect, the de-esser effect, or the de-clicker effect, to fix any errors, glitches, or inconsistencies in your podcast audio.

- Optimize your podcast audio for the best sound quality and consistency. You can use the editing software's tools, such as the normalize tool, the level tool, or the loudness tool, to optimize your podcast audio for the best sound quality and consistency. You can also use the editing software's effects, such as the compressor effect, the equalizer effect, or the limiter effect, to optimize your podcast audio for the best sound quality and consistency.

- Export your podcast audio in the right format and quality. You can use the editing software's tools, such as the export tool, the save tool, or the render tool, to export your podcast audio in the right format and quality. You can also use the editing software's settings, such as the format settings, the quality settings, or the metadata settings, to export your podcast audio in the right format and quality. You should choose the right format, such as MP3, WAV, or AAC, depending on your podcast platform and audience. You should also choose the right quality, such as bitrate, sample rate, or channels, depending on your audio content and size. You should also add information and details to your podcast audio file, such as the title, the description, the artwork, or the tags.

CHAPTER 6: DISTRIBUTION AND PLATFORMS

After you have edited and produced your podcast with the right tools and techniques, the next step is to distribute and publish your podcast with the right platforms and strategies. Distributing and publishing your podcast will help you reach and grow your audience, and also increase your visibility and credibility as a podcaster. In this chapter, we will cover the following topics:

- Understanding podcast hosting platforms
- Submitting your podcast to major directories (Apple Podcasts, Spotify, Google Podcasts, etc.)
- Leveraging social media for promotion

Understanding podcast hosting platforms

A podcast hosting platform is a service that stores and delivers your podcast audio files to your listeners. It also provides you with an RSS feed, which is a link that contains information and details about your podcast, such as the title, description, artwork, and episodes. You need an RSS feed to submit your podcast to directories and aggregators, which are the platforms that allow your listeners to find and subscribe to your podcast.

There are many podcast hosting platforms available, each with different features, functions, and prices. You should choose a podcast hosting platform that meets your needs, your budget, and your goals. Some of the factors to consider when choosing a podcast hosting platform are:

- **Storage space:** How much space do you need to store your podcast audio files? Some podcast hosting platforms offer unlimited storage, while others have limits or charge extra fees for additional space.

- **Bandwidth:** How much bandwidth do you need to deliver your podcast audio files to your listeners? Bandwidth is the amount of data that can be transferred in a given time. Some podcast hosting platforms offer unlimited bandwidth, while others have limits or charge extra fees for additional bandwidth.

- **Analytics:** How much analytics do you need to track and measure your podcast performance? Analytics are the data and insights that show you how your podcast is doing, such as the number of downloads, listens, subscribers, and reviews. Some podcast hosting platforms offer basic analytics, while others offer advanced analytics or integrate with third-party tools.

- **Support:** How much support do you need to set up and manage your podcast? Support is the help and guidance that the podcast hosting platform provides you, such as tutorials, FAQs, forums, or customer service. Some podcast hosting platforms offer more support than others, depending on their level of expertise and availability.

Some of the best podcast hosting platforms are:

- **bCast**: A podcast hosting, distribution, and analytics platform designed to transform listeners into leads. It is good for podcasters who want to grow their audience and generate income from their podcast. It offers unlimited storage, bandwidth, and analytics, as well as features such as dynamic content insertion, transcription, and email capture. It also integrates with popular tools such as Zapier, WordPress, and Mailchimp.

bCast

- **Buzzsprout**: A podcast hosting, distribution, and analytics platform that is easy to use and affordable. It is good for podcasters who want to start and grow their podcast with minimal hassle and cost. It offers 250 GB of bandwidth per month, basic analytics, and features such as episode scheduling, chapter markers, and magic mastering. It also integrates with popular directories such as Apple Podcasts, Spotify, and Google Podcasts. Buzzsprout

- **Transistor**: A podcast hosting, distribution, and analytics platform that is professional and reliable. It is good for podcasters who want to create and manage multiple podcasts with high quality and performance. It offers unlimited storage, bandwidth, and analytics, as well as features such as branded websites, private podcasts, and team accounts. It also integrates with popular tools such as Stripe, ConvertKit, and Chartable. Transistor

- **Anchor**: A podcast hosting, distribution, and analytics platform that is free and user-friendly. It is good for podcasters who want to create and publish their podcast with ease and convenience. It offers unlimited storage, bandwidth, and analytics, as well as features such as episode creation, monetization, and distribution. It also integrates with popular directories such as Apple Podcasts, Spotify, and Google Podcasts. Anchor

Submitting your podcast to major directories (Apple Podcasts, Spotify, Google Podcasts, etc.)

A podcast directory is a platform that allows listeners to find and subscribe to podcasts. It is also a platform that allows podcasters to distribute and promote their podcasts. There are many podcast directories available, each with different features, functions, and audiences. You should submit your podcast to as many podcast directories as possible, to increase your reach and exposure as a podcaster.

Some of the factors to consider when submitting your podcast to podcast directories are:

- **Requirements**: What are the requirements to submit your podcast to the podcast directory? Some podcast directories have specific requirements, such as the format, quality, or size of your podcast audio files, or the information and details of your podcast RSS feed. You should make sure that your podcast meets the requirements of the podcast directory before submitting it.

- **Process**: What is the process to submit your podcast to the podcast directory? Some podcast directories have different processes, such as the steps, tools, or platforms that you need to use to submit your podcast. You should follow the process of the podcast directory carefully and accurately to submit your podcast successfully.

- **Approval**: What is the approval time and criteria for your podcast to be listed on the podcast directory? Some podcast directories have different approval times and criteria, such as the duration, frequency, or standards that they use to review and approve your podcast. You should be patient and prepared for the approval time and criteria of the podcast directory.

Some of the best podcast directories are:

- **Apple Podcasts:** The largest and most popular podcast directory in the world. It is good for podcasters who want to reach a massive and loyal audience of podcast listeners. It requires your podcast audio files to be in MP3, AAC, or WAV format, and your podcast RSS feed to have a title, description, artwork, and category. It also requires you to have an Apple ID and use iTunes or Podcasts Connect to submit your podcast. It usually takes up to 5 days to approve your podcast. Apple

Podcasts

- **Spotify**: The second largest and fastest-growing podcast directory in the world. It is good for podcasters who want to reach a young and diverse audience of podcast listeners. It requires your podcast audio files to be in MP3, M4A, or OGG format, and your podcast RSS feed to have a title, description, artwork, and language. It also requires you to have a Spotify account and use Spotify for Podcasters to submit your podcast. It usually takes up to 24 hours to approve your podcast. [Spotify]

- **Google Podcasts:** The third largest and most accessible podcast directory in the world. It is good for podcasters who want to reach an Android and Google-friendly audience of podcast listeners. It requires your podcast audio files to be in MP3, M4A, or OGG format, and your podcast RSS feed to have a title, description, artwork, and language. It also requires you to have a Google account and use Google Podcasts Manager to submit your podcast. It usually takes up to 24 hours to approve your podcast. [Google Podcasts]

- **Amazon Music:** The newest and most ambitious podcast directory in the world. It is good for podcasters who want to reach an Amazon and Alexa-friendly audience of podcast listeners. It requires your podcast audio files to be in MP3, M4A, or OGG format, and your podcast RSS feed to have a title, description, artwork, and language. It also requires you to have an Amazon account and use Amazon Music for Podcasters to submit your podcast. It usually takes up to 24 hours to approve your podcast. [Amazon Music]

CHAPTER 7: PROMOTION AND MARKETING

After you have distributed and published your podcast with the right platforms and strategies, the next step is to promote and market your podcast with the right tools and techniques. Promoting and marketing your podcast will help you attract and retain your audience, and also increase your revenue and reputation as a podcaster. In this chapter, we will cover the following topics:

- Building a website for your podcast
- Utilizing social media marketing strategies
- Collaborating with other podcasters and influencers
- Using email marketing for audience engagement

Building a website for your podcast

A website is a platform that allows you to display and share your podcast online. It is also a platform that allows you to provide more information and value to your audience, such as show notes, transcripts, resources, or blog posts. A website can also help you improve your podcast's SEO, branding, and monetization.

There are many ways to build a website for your podcast, depending on your needs, budget, and skills. You can use a website builder, such as Squarespace, Wix, or WordPress, to create a website for your podcast without coding. You can also use a podcast hosting platform, such as bCast, Buzzsprout, or Transistor, to create a website for your podcast with their templates and features. You can also use a custom domain, such as yourpodcast.com, to create a website for your podcast with your own design and functionality.

Some of the best practices for building a website for your podcast are:

- Choose a domain name that is relevant, memorable, and easy to spell and pronounce. You can use your podcast name, your niche, or your keywords as your domain name. You can also use a domain name generator, such as Namecheap, GoDaddy, or Domain.com, to find and register a domain name for your podcast.

- Design a logo and a color scheme that represents your podcast and your brand. You can use a logo maker, such as Canva, LogoMaker, or Tailor Brands, to create a logo for your podcast. You can also use a color picker, such as Coolors, Adobe Color, or Paletton, to choose a color scheme for your podcast.

- Create a homepage that introduces your podcast and your value proposition. You can use a headline, a subheadline, and a call to action to capture your audience's attention and interest. You can also use an image, a video, or an audio player to display your podcast and your content.

- Create a podcast page that displays your podcast episodes and your show notes. You can use a podcast player, such as Smart Podcast Player, Fusebox, or Podcorn, to embed your podcast episodes on your website. You can also use show notes, such as summaries, transcripts, resources, or links, to provide more information and value to your audience.

- Create a blog page that publishes your blog posts and your content. You can use a blog platform, such as

Medium, Substack, or Ghost, to write and publish your blog posts. You can also use content, such as articles, guides, tips, or stories, to educate, entertain, or inspire your audience.

. Create an about page that tells your story and your mission. You can use a bio, a photo, and a contact form to introduce yourself and your podcast. You can also use a mission statement, a vision statement, or a value statement to share your goals and your purpose.

. Create a subscribe page that encourages your audience to subscribe to your podcast and your email list. You can use a subscribe button, a sign-up form, or a lead magnet to collect your audience's email addresses and send them updates, newsletters, or offers. You can also use a social media button, a review button, or a share button to invite your audience to follow, rate, or share your podcast.

Utilizing social media marketing strategies

Social media is a platform that allows you to create and share content and interact with your audience. It is also a platform that allows you to promote and market your podcast to new and existing listeners. There are many social media platforms available, each with different features, functions, and audiences. You should utilize social media marketing strategies to increase your awareness and engagement as a podcaster.

Some of the factors to consider when utilizing social media marketing strategies are:

. **Strategy**: What is your strategy to market your podcast on social media? You should have a clear and specific strategy, such as the goals, objectives, and metrics that you want to achieve with your social media marketing. You should also have a plan, such as the content, channels, and schedule that you want to use for your social media marketing.

- **Content**: What is your content to market your podcast on social media? You should have a variety of content, such as text, images, videos, or audio clips, that highlight your podcast and entice your audience. You should also have a value proposition, such as the benefits, features, or solutions that your podcast offers to your audience.

- **Channels**: What are your channels to market your podcast on social media? You should have a mix of channels, such as Facebook, Twitter, Instagram, or LinkedIn, that suit your podcast and your audience. You should also have a profile, such as a name, bio, logo, or link, that represents your podcast and your brand.

- **Schedule**: What is your schedule to market your podcast on social media? You should have a consistent and frequent schedule, such as the days, times, and frequency that you post your content on social media. You should also have a calendar, such as a spreadsheet, a tool, or an app, that helps you organize and manage your social media marketing.

Some of the best practices for utilizing social media marketing strategies are:

- **Be authentic and transparent.** You should be yourself and share your story, your personality, and your passion with your audience. You should also be honest and open about your podcast, your goals, and your challenges. This will help you build trust and rapport with your audience and make them feel more connected to you and your podcast.

- **Be engaging and interactive.** You should not only post your content, but also engage and interact with your audience. You should respond to their comments, questions, and feedback, and also initiate conversations, polls, or contests. This will help you create a community and a loyal fan base around your podcast, and also get valuable insights and suggestions from your audience.

- **Be consistent and relevant.** You should not only post frequently, but also post quality and relevant content. You should post content that matches your podcast's niche, format, and tone, and that also provides value, entertainment, or education to your audience. You should also post content that is timely, trendy, or seasonal, and that also aligns with your podcast's goals and objectives.

- **Be creative and innovative.** You should not only post the same type of content, but also experiment and try new things. You should use different formats, such as images, videos, or audio clips, and different elements, such as stories, examples, facts, statistics, quotes, or testimonials, to make your content more interesting and varied. You should also use different tools, such as graphic design, video editing, or audio editing, to make your content more professional and polished.

Collaborating with other podcasters and influencers

Collaborating with other podcasters and influencers is a strategy that allows you to network and partner with other people who have similar or complementary podcasts, niches, or audiences. It is also a strategy that allows you to cross-promote and co-create content and value for your listeners. Collaborating with other podcasters and influencers can help you expand your reach and exposure as a podcaster, and also increase your credibility and authority as a podcaster.

There are many ways to collaborate with other podcasters and influencers, depending on your needs, goals, and relationships. You can use podcast guesting, a podcast swap, or a podcast interview to collaborate with other podcasters and influencers. You can also use a podcast roundup, a podcast review, or a podcast recommendation to collaborate with other podcasters and influencers.

Some of the best practices for collaborating with other podcasters and influencers are:

- Find the right podcasters and influencers to collaborate with. You should find podcasters and influencers who have similar or complementary podcasts, niches, or audiences, and who also have a good reputation, a large following, or a high engagement. You can use a podcast directory, such as Apple Podcasts, Spotify, or Google Podcasts, to find podcasters and influencers who are relevant to your podcast. You can also use a podcast search engine, such as Listen Notes, Podchaser, or Chartable, to find podcasters and influencers who are popular or influential in your podcast.

- Reach out to the podcasters and influencers you want to collaborate with. You should reach out to the podcasters and influencers you want to collaborate with in a polite, professional, and personalized way. You should introduce yourself and your podcast, explain why you want to collaborate with them, and propose a collaboration idea that is beneficial for both parties. You can use an email, a social media message, or a podcast mention to reach out to the podcasters and influencers you want to collaborate with. You can also use a podcast booking platform, such as PodcastGuests, MatchMaker, or Podcorn, to reach out to the podcasters and influencers you want to collaborate with.

- Deliver value and quality to the podcasters and influencers you collaborate with. You should deliver value and quality to the podcasters and influencers you collaborate with in a respectful, reliable, and reciprocal way. You should prepare well and perform well for the collaboration, whether it is a podcast guesting, a podcast swap, or a podcast interview. You should also promote and support the collaboration, whether it is a podcast roundup, a podcast review, or a podcast recommendation.

Using email marketing for audience engagement

Email marketing is a strategy that allows you to communicate and connect with your audience via email. It is also a strategy that allows you to provide more information and value to your audience, such as updates, newsletters, or offers. Email marketing can help you increase your audience engagement and retention as a podcaster, and also increase your revenue and conversion as a podcaster.

There are many ways to use email marketing for audience engagement, depending on your needs, goals, and resources. You can use an email list, an email service provider, or an email marketing platform to use email marketing for audience engagement. You can also use email capture, an email campaign, or email automation to use email marketing for audience engagement.

Some of the best practices for using email marketing for audience engagement are:

- Build an email list of your podcast listeners. You should build an email list of your podcast listeners who are interested in receiving more information and value from you via email. You can use an email capture, such as a sign-up form, a lead magnet, or a call to action, to collect your podcast listeners' email addresses and permission to email them. You can also use a podcast hosting platform, such as bCast, Buzzsprout, or Transistor, to collect your podcast listeners' email addresses and permission to email them.

- Choose an email service provider or an email marketing platform to manage your email list and send your emails. You should choose an email service provider or an email marketing platform that meets your needs, your budget, and your goals. You can use an email service provider, such as Mailchimp, ConvertKit, or AWeber, to manage your email list and send your emails. You can also use an email marketing platform, such as PodInbox, Substack, or Revue, to manage your email list and send your emails.

- Create and send email campaigns that provide value and engagement to your podcast listeners. You should create and send email campaigns that provide value and engagement to your podcast listeners, such as updates, newsletters, or offers. You can use an email campaign, such as a welcome email, a new episode email, or a feedback email, to provide value and engagement to your podcast listeners. You can also use email automation, such as a drip campaign, a nurture campaign, or a re-engagement campaign, to provide value and engagement to your podcast listeners.

CHAPTER 8: MONETIZATION STRATEGIES

One of the most exciting and challenging aspects of podcasting is monetizing your podcast. Monetizing your podcast means generating income from your podcast, either directly or indirectly. Monetizing your podcast can help you cover your costs, reward your efforts, and grow your podcast.

There are many monetization models and strategies available for podcasters, depending on your niche, audience, and goals. You should explore different monetization models and strategies and find the ones that work best for you and your podcast. In this chapter, we will cover the following topics:

- Exploring different monetization models (ads, sponsorships, donations, etc.)
- Setting up affiliate marketing for your podcast
- Tips for maximizing revenue

Exploring different monetization models (ads, sponsorships, donations, etc.)

A monetization model is a way of generating income from your podcast, either directly or indirectly. A direct monetization model means that you receive money from your listeners or customers, such as through subscriptions, donations, or products. An indirect monetization model means that you receive money from third parties, such as through ads, sponsorships, or partnerships.

There are many monetization models available for podcasters, each with different advantages, disadvantages, and requirements. You should explore different monetization models, and find the ones that suit your podcast's niche, format, and tone, and that also provide value, convenience, and satisfaction to your listeners. Some of the most common and popular monetization models are:

- **Ads**: Ads are short audio clips that promote a product, service, or brand, and that are inserted into your podcast episodes, usually at the beginning, middle, or end. Ads are one of the easiest and most common ways to monetize a podcast, as they require little or no upfront cost, and they can generate a steady and passive income. However, ads can also be annoying and intrusive for your listeners, and they can also lower your podcast's quality and credibility, especially if they are irrelevant or excessive. To use ads as a monetization model, you need to have a large and loyal audience, and you also need to find and negotiate with advertisers, either directly or through an ad network, such as AdvertiseCast, Midroll, or Podcorn.

- **Sponsorships**: Sponsorships are long-term and mutually beneficial relationships between you and a sponsor, who is a company or an organization that supports your podcast financially or in-kind, in exchange for exposure, endorsement, or affiliation. Sponsorships are one of the most lucrative and prestigious ways to monetize a podcast, as they can generate a high and consistent income, and they can also boost your podcast's quality and authority, especially if they are relevant and reputable. However, sponsorships can also be difficult and demanding to obtain and maintain, as they require a lot of trust, communication, and performance, and they can also limit your podcast's creativity and independence, especially if they are restrictive or exclusive. To use sponsorships as a monetization model, you need to have a niche and engaged audience, and you also need to find and pitch to sponsors, either directly or through a sponsorship platform, such as Podcorn, PodGrid, or Podcorn.

- **Donations**: Donations are voluntary and generous contributions from your listeners or supporters, who give you money or other resources, such as feedback, reviews, or referrals, to show their appreciation, gratitude, or loyalty. Donations are one of the most simple and flexible ways to monetize a podcast, as they require no or low upfront cost, and they can generate a variable and active income. However, donations can also be unpredictable and unreliable, as they depend on your listeners' willingness and ability to pay, and they can also be insufficient and unsustainable, especially if they are sporadic or low. To use donations as a monetization model, you need to have a passionate and loyal audience, and you also need to ask and thank your listeners, either directly or through a donation platform, such as Patreon, Buy Me a Coffee, or PodFan.

Setting up affiliate marketing for your podcast

Affiliate marketing is a way of generating income from your podcast by promoting other people's products or services, and receiving a commission for each sale or action that you refer. Affiliate marketing is one of the most effective and popular ways to monetize a podcast, as it can generate a high and scalable income, and it can also provide value and relevance to your listeners, especially if you promote products or services that are related to your podcast's niche or topic.

There are many ways to set up affiliate marketing for your podcast, depending on your needs, goals, and resources. You can use an affiliate program, an affiliate network, or an affiliate platform to set up affiliate marketing for your podcast. You can also use an affiliate link, an affiliate code, or an affiliate banner to set up affiliate marketing for your podcast.

Some of the best practices for setting up affiliate marketing for your podcast are:

- Find the right products or services to promote on your podcast. You should find products or services that are relevant, useful, and valuable to your podcast's niche or topic, and that also have a good reputation, a high commission, or a high conversion rate. You can use an affiliate program, such as Amazon Associates, Fiverr, or ExpressVPN , to find products or services that are related to your podcast. You can also use an affiliate network, such as ShareASale, CJ Affiliate, or ClickBank , to find products or services that are popular or profitable in your podcast.

- Create and share your affiliate links, codes, or banners on your podcast. You should create and share your affiliate links, codes, or banners on your podcast in a clear, honest, and persuasive way. You should use an affiliate link, such as yourpodcast.com/product, yourpodcast.com/recommends/product, or product.com/yourpodcast, to direct your listeners to the product or service's website. You should also use an affiliate code, such as YOURPODCAST, YOURPODCAST10, or YOURPODCAST20, to give your listeners a discount or a bonus when they purchase the product or service. You should also use an affiliate banner, such as an image, a video, or an audio clip, to display or play the product or service's logo, name, or slogan on your podcast.

- Track and optimize your affiliate marketing performance on your podcast. You should track and optimize your affiliate marketing performance on your podcast in a smart, data-driven, and strategic way. You should use an affiliate platform, such as Pretty Links, ThirstyAffiliates, or Podcorn , to manage, track, and optimize your affiliate links, codes, or banners on your podcast. You should also use analytics, such as downloads, clicks, sales, or commissions, to measure, analyze, and improve your affiliate marketing results on your podcast.

Tips for maximizing revenue

Monetizing your podcast is not a one-time or a one-way process. It is a continuous and a multi-way process that requires constant testing, learning, and improving. To maximize your revenue from your podcast, you should not rely on a single monetization model or strategy, but rather diversify and combine different monetization models and strategies, such as ads, sponsorships, donations, affiliate marketing, and more.

Some of the tips for maximizing revenue from your podcast are:

- Know your audience and your value. You should know your audience and your value and use them as your guide and your leverage for monetizing your podcast. You should know your audience's demographics, preferences, and behaviors, and use them to tailor your monetization models and strategies to their needs, wants, and expectations. You should also know your value proposition, your unique selling point, and your competitive advantage, and use them to differentiate your podcast from others, and to justify your monetization models and strategies to your listeners and your partners.

- Grow your audience and your influence. You should grow your audience and your influence and use them as your foundation and your catalyst for monetizing your podcast. You should grow your audience's size, engagement, and loyalty, and use them to increase your podcast's reach, exposure, and retention. You should also grow your influence's reputation, authority, and credibility, and use them to increase your podcast's quality, trust, and respect.

- Experiment and optimize your monetization models and strategies. You should experiment and optimize your monetization models and strategies and use them as your tool and your opportunity for monetizing your podcast. You should experiment with different monetization models and strategies, such as ads, sponsorships, donations, affiliate marketing, and more, and use them to find the best fit and the best mix for your podcast and your audience. You should also optimize your monetization models and strategies, such as by testing, measuring, analyzing, and improving your monetization performance, and use them to find the best way and the best time to monetize your podcast and your audience.

CHAPTER 9: GROWING AND ENGAGING YOUR AUDIENCE

One of the most rewarding and challenging aspects of podcasting is growing and engaging your audience. Growing your audience means attracting and acquiring more listeners for your podcast, either organically or strategically. Engaging your audience means communicating and connecting with your listeners and providing them with more information and value. Growing and engaging your audience can help you increase your podcast's reach, exposure, and retention, and also increase your podcast's quality, trust, and respect.

There are many tools and techniques available for podcasters to grow and engage their audience, depending on your niche, audience, and goals. You should use different tools and techniques to grow and engage your audience and find the ones that work best for you and your podcast. In this chapter, we will cover the following topics:

- Building a community around your podcast
- Leveraging listener feedback and reviews
- Strategies for audience retention and growth

Building a community around your podcast

A community is a group of people who share a common interest, passion, or purpose, and who interact and support each other. A community can also be a platform that allows you to display and share your podcast, and to provide more information and value to your listeners, such as show notes, transcripts, resources, or blog posts. Building a community around your podcast can help you grow and engage your audience, and also increase your podcast's loyalty, advocacy, and referrals.

There are many ways to build a community around your podcast, depending on your needs, goals, and resources. You can use a website, a social media platform, or a community platform to build a community around your podcast. You can also use a forum, a chat, or a group to build a community around your podcast.

Some of the best practices for building a community around your podcast are:

- Choose a platform that suits your podcast and your audience. You should choose a platform that meets your needs, your budget, and your goals. You should also choose a platform that suits your podcast's niche, format, and tone, and that also provides value, convenience, and satisfaction to your listeners. You can use a website, such as Squarespace, Wix, or WordPress, to create a website for your podcast. You can also use a social media platform, such as Facebook, Twitter, Instagram, or LinkedIn, to create a social media page or profile for your podcast. You can also use a community platform, such as Discord, Slack, or Mighty Networks, to create a community platform for your podcast.

- Create and share content that provides value and engagement to your listeners. You should create and share content that provides value and engagement to your listeners, such as show notes, transcripts, resources, or blog posts. You should also create and share content that matches your podcast's niche, format, and tone, and that also provides education, entertainment, or inspiration to your listeners. You can use a podcast player, such as Smart Podcast Player,

Fusebox, or Podcorn, to embed your podcast episodes on your platform. You can also use show notes, such as summaries, transcripts, resources, or links, to provide more information and value to your listeners. You can also use blog posts, such as articles, guides, tips, or stories, to provide more content and value to your listeners.

· Encourage and facilitate interaction and support among your listeners. You should encourage and facilitate interaction and support among your listeners and create a sense of community and belonging. You should respond to their comments, questions, and feedback, and also initiate conversations, polls, or contests. You should also invite them to share their opinions, experiences, or stories, and also acknowledge, appreciate, or reward them. You can use a forum, such as Reddit, Quora, or Stack Exchange, to create a forum for your podcast. You can also use a chat, such as Telegram, WhatsApp, or Signal, to create a chat for your podcast. You can also use a group, such as Facebook Group, LinkedIn Group, or Meetup, to create a group for your podcast.

Leveraging listener feedback and reviews

Listener feedback and reviews are comments, ratings, or testimonials from your listeners or customers, who give you their opinions, suggestions, or praises. Listener feedback and reviews can also be a source of information and value for your potential listeners or customers, who look for your reputation, credibility, or quality. Leveraging listener feedback and reviews can help you grow and engage your audience, and also increase your podcast's improvement, innovation, and conversion.

There are many ways to leverage listener feedback and reviews, depending on your needs, goals, and resources. You can use a survey, a form, or a tool to collect listener feedback and reviews. You can also use a directory, a platform, or a website to display listener feedback and reviews.

Some of the best practices for leveraging listener feedback and reviews are:

- Ask for listener feedback and reviews in a clear, honest, and persuasive way. You should ask for listener feedback and reviews in a clear, honest, and persuasive way, and explain why you need them, how you will use them, and what they will get in return. You should also ask for listener feedback and reviews at the right time, such as at the end of your podcast episode, after they have listened to your podcast, or when they are most likely to give you feedback or reviews. You can use a survey, such as SurveyMonkey, Google Forms, or Typeform, to create a survey for your podcast. You can also use a form, such as Podchaser, Podcorn, or PodInbox, to create a form for your podcast. You can also use a tool, such as Podcorn, PodGrid, or Podcorn, to create a tool for your podcast.

- Analyze and act on listener feedback and reviews in a smart, data-driven, and strategic way. You should analyze and act on listener feedback and reviews in a smart, data-driven, and strategic way, and use them to improve, innovate, or optimize your podcast. You should also acknowledge and appreciate listener feedback and reviews, and show them that you value their opinions, suggestions, or praises. You can use analytics, such as downloads, ratings, reviews, or comments, to measure, analyze, and improve your podcast performance. You can also use insights, such as strengths, weaknesses, opportunities, or threats, to identify, prioritize, and implement your podcast improvements.

- Highlight and share listener feedback and reviews in a clear, attractive, and compelling way. You should showcase and share listener feedback and reviews in a clear, attractive, and compelling way, and use them to promote, market, or sell your podcast. You should also encourage and incentivize listener feedback and reviews, and make them easy, convenient, and rewarding for your listeners. You can use a directory, such as Apple Podcasts, Spotify, or Google Podcasts, to display your podcast ratings and reviews. You can also use a platform, such as Podchaser, Chartable, or Podcorn, to display your podcast ratings and reviews. You can also use a website, such as your own website, a testimonial website, or a review website, to display your podcast ratings and reviews.

Strategies for audience retention and growth

Audience retention and growth are two key metrics that measure your podcast's success and potential. Audience retention means keeping your existing listeners loyal, engaged, and satisfied. Audience growth means acquiring new listeners organically, strategically, or virally. Both audience retention and growth can help you increase your podcast's reach, exposure, and retention, and also increase your podcast's quality, trust, and respect.

There are many strategies for audience retention and growth, depending on your niche, audience, and goals. You should use different strategies for audience retention and growth and find the ones that work best for you and your podcast. Some of the most effective and popular strategies for audience retention and growth are:

- Provide consistent and quality content. You should provide consistent and quality content and deliver it on a regular and predictable schedule. You should also provide content that matches your podcast's niche, format, and tone, and that also provides value, entertainment, or education to your listeners. You can use a content calendar, such as a spreadsheet, a tool, or an app, to plan, organize, and manage your content. You can also use a content strategy, such as a mission statement, a vision statement, or a value statement, to guide, align, and optimize your content.

- Optimize your podcast for discovery and SEO. You should optimize your podcast for discovery and SEO and make it easy and convenient for your potential listeners to find and subscribe to your podcast. You should also optimize your podcast for different platforms, directories, and devices, and make it compatible and accessible for your listeners. You can use keywords, such as your podcast name, your niche, or your topic, to optimize your podcast title, description, and tags. You can also use metadata, such as your podcast artwork, category, and language, to optimize your podcast RSS feed and show page.

- Promote and market your podcast effectively and creatively. You should promote and market your podcast effectively and creatively, and use different channels, methods, and techniques to reach and attract your potential listeners. You should also promote and market your podcast to your target audience, and use different messages, offers, and incentives to persuade and convert them. You can use social media, such as Facebook, Twitter, Instagram, or LinkedIn, to promote and market your podcast. You can also use email marketing, such as Mailchimp, ConvertKit, or AWeber, to promote and market your podcast. You can also use podcast cross-promotion, such as podcast guesting.

CHAPTER 10: ADAPTING TO TRENDS AND TECHNOLOGIES

Podcasting is a dynamic and evolving medium, influenced by changing listener preferences, technology integration, and industry innovation. As a podcaster, you need to adapt to trends and technologies, and stay updated and relevant in the podcasting landscape. Adapting to trends and technologies can help you improve your podcast's quality, performance, and potential, and also increase your podcast's creativity, diversity, and impact.

There are many sources and resources available for podcasters to adapt to trends and technologies, depending on your needs, goals, and interests. You should use different sources and resources to adapt to trends and technologies and find the ones that work best for you and your podcast. In this chapter, we will cover the following topics:

- Staying updated on the latest podcasting tools and software
- Incorporating emerging trends in the podcasting landscape

Staying updated on the latest podcasting tools and software

Podcasting tools and software are the applications and programs that you use to create, edit, distribute, and manage your podcast. Podcasting tools and software can also enhance your podcast's functionality, accessibility, and analytics. Staying updated on the latest podcasting tools and software can help you optimize your podcasting workflow, and also increase your podcast's efficiency, effectiveness, and quality.

There are many podcasting tools and software available for podcasters, each with different features, functions, and prices. You should stay updated on the latest podcasting tools and software, and find the ones that suit your podcast's needs, budget, and goals. Some of the most common and popular podcasting tools and software are:

- Recording tools and software: Recording tools and software are the applications and programs that you use to capture and record your podcast audio. Recording tools and software can also help you improve your podcast's sound quality, clarity, and consistency. You can use a microphone, such as Blue Yeti, Rode PodMic, or Shure SM7B, to capture your podcast audio. You can also use a recorder, such as Zoom H6, Tascam DR-40X, or Rodecaster Pro, to record your podcast audio.

- Editing tools and software: Editing tools and software are the applications and programs that you use to edit and polish your podcast audio. Editing tools and software can also help you enhance your podcast's sound effects, transitions, and music. You can use editing software, such as Audacity, GarageBand, or Adobe Audition, to edit your podcast audio. You can also use an editing tool, such as Descript, Alitu, or Hindenburg Journalist, to edit your podcast audio.

- Hosting tools and software: Hosting tools and software are the applications and programs that you use to host and store your podcast audio files. Hosting tools and software can also help you distribute and syndicate your podcast to different platforms and directories. You can use a hosting platform, such as bCast, Buzzsprout, or Transistor, to host your podcast audio files. You can also use a hosting tool, such as Podcorn, PodGrid, or Podcorn, to host your podcast audio files.

- Management tools and software: Management tools and software are the applications and programs that you use to manage and monitor your podcast performance and growth. Management tools and software can also help you analyze and optimize your podcast metrics and feedback. You can use a management platform, such as Podchaser, Chartable, or Podcorn, to manage your podcast performance and growth. You can also use a management tool, such as Pretty Links, ThirstyAffiliates, or Podcorn, to manage your podcast performance and growth.

Incorporating emerging trends in the podcasting landscape

Podcasting trends are the patterns and movements that shape and influence the podcasting industry and culture. Podcasting trends can also reflect and respond to the changing listener preferences, technology integration, and industry innovation. Incorporating emerging trends in the podcasting landscape can help you stay updated and relevant in the podcasting industry and culture, and also increase your podcast's creativity, diversity, and impact.

There are many emerging trends in the podcasting landscape, each with different implications and opportunities for podcasters. You should incorporate emerging trends in the podcasting landscape, and find the ones that suit your podcast's niche, format, and tone. Some of the most emerging trends in the podcasting landscape are:

- **Podcast advertising and monetization**: Podcast advertising and monetization are the ways and means of generating income from your podcast, either directly or indirectly. Podcast advertising and monetization are becoming more popular and profitable, as more listeners, advertisers, and sponsors are willing to pay for podcast content and exposure. You can use ads, sponsorships, donations, or affiliate marketing to monetize your podcast. You can also use subscriptions, products, or services to monetize your podcast.

- **Podcast discovery and SEO**: Podcast discovery and SEO are the ways and means of making your podcast easy and convenient to find and subscribe to by your potential listeners. Podcast discovery and SEO are becoming more important and challenging, as more podcasts, platforms, and directories are competing for listener attention and loyalty. You can use keywords, metadata, or RSS feed to optimize your podcast for discovery and SEO. You can also use social media, email marketing, or podcast cross-promotion to optimize your podcast for discovery and SEO.

CHAPTER 11: TROUBLESHOOTING AND COMMON CHALLENGES

Podcasting is a rewarding and fulfilling medium, but it also comes with its own set of challenges and difficulties. As a podcaster, you may encounter technical issues, burnout, or legal considerations that can affect your podcast's quality, performance, and potential. Troubleshooting and overcoming these common challenges can help you improve your podcasting skills, experience, and results, and also increase your podcast's efficiency, effectiveness, and quality.

There are many sources and resources available for podcasters to troubleshoot and overcome common challenges, depending on your needs, goals, and interests. You should use different sources and resources to troubleshoot and overcome common challenges and find the ones that work best for you and your podcast. In this chapter, we will cover the following topics:

- Addressing technical issues
- Dealing with burnout
- Navigating copyright and legal considerations

Addressing technical issues

Technical issues are the problems and errors that you may

encounter with your podcasting tools and software, such as recording, editing, hosting, or management. Technical issues can affect your podcast's sound quality, functionality, or accessibility, and can also cause frustration, stress, or delay. Addressing technical issues can help you optimize your podcasting workflow, and also increase your podcast's reliability, compatibility, and quality.

There are many ways to address technical issues, depending on your needs, goals, and resources. You can use troubleshooting guides, tutorials, or articles to address technical issues. You can also use forums, chats, or groups to address technical issues.

Some of the best practices for addressing technical issues are:

- Identify and diagnose the technical issue. You should identify and diagnose the technical issue, and determine its cause, effect, and solution. You should also check if the technical issue is related to your podcasting tool or software, your device or system, or your internet or network. You can use troubleshooting guides, such as How to Fix 8 Common Podcast Audio Issues, [Podcast Troubleshooting: How to Fix Common Problems], or [Podcast Troubleshooting: 5 Common Problems and How to Fix Them], to identify and diagnose the technical issue.

- Search and apply the solution for the technical issue. You should search and apply the solution for the technical issue, and test if it works, or if it causes any other problems. You should also backup your podcast files and data and update your podcasting tools and software regularly. You can use tutorials or articles, such as [How to Record a Podcast], [How to Edit a Podcast], or [How to Host a Podcast], to search and apply the solution for the technical issue.

- Seek and receive help for the technical issue. You should seek and receive help for the technical issue, and ask for advice, feedback, or support from other podcasters or experts. You should also share your experience, knowledge, or tips with other podcasters or beginners who may face the same or similar technical issues. You can use forums, chats, or groups, such as [r/podcasting], [Podcasters' Support Group], or [Podcast Movement Community], to seek and receive help for the technical issue.

- Prevent and avoid future technical issues. You should prevent and avoid future technical issues, and learn from your mistakes, challenges, or successes. You should also invest in quality podcasting tools and software and maintain them properly and regularly. You can use reviews, ratings, or recommendations, such as [The Best Podcasting Microphones], [The Best Podcast Editing Software], or [The Best Podcast Hosting Platforms], to prevent and avoid future technical issues. You can also use checklists, templates, or workflows, such as [The Podcast Recording Checklist], [The Podcast Editing Template], or [The Podcast Publishing Workflow], to prevent and avoid future technical issues.

Dealing with burnout

Burnout is the state of physical, mental, or emotional exhaustion that you may experience as a result of prolonged or excessive stress, pressure, or workload. Burnout can affect your podcast's quality, performance, or potential, and can also cause dissatisfaction, frustration, or depression. Dealing with burnout can help you restore your energy, motivation, and passion, and also increase your podcast's enjoyment, fulfillment, and quality.

There are many ways to deal with burnout, depending on your needs, goals, and resources. You can use self-care, relaxation, or hobbies to deal with burnout. You can also use planning, delegation, or collaboration to deal with burnout.

Some of the best practices for dealing with burnout are:

- Recognize and acknowledge the signs and symptoms

of burnout. You should recognize and acknowledge the signs and symptoms of burnout and understand how they affect you and your podcast. You should also be honest and realistic about your podcast's expectations, challenges, and achievements. You can use self-assessment tools, such as [The Podcast Burnout Quiz], [The Podcast Burnout Assessment], or [The Podcast Burnout Scale], to recognize and acknowledge the signs and symptoms of burnout.

- Take care of yourself and your well-being. You should take care of yourself and your well-being, and prioritize your physical, mental, and emotional health. You should also balance your podcasting and personal life, and set boundaries and limits for your podcasting time, energy, and resources. You can use self-care, relaxation, or hobbies, such as exercise, meditation, or reading, to take care of yourself and your well-being.

- Seek and receive support and encouragement. You should seek and receive support and encouragement, and ask for help, advice, or feedback from your family, friends, or peers. You should also appreciate and celebrate your podcast's progress, success, or impact, and acknowledge and reward your podcasting efforts, contributions, or achievements. You can use planning, delegation, or collaboration, such as scheduling, outsourcing, or partnering, to seek and receive support and encouragement.

- Reevaluate and redefine your podcasting goals and vision. You should reevaluate and redefine your podcasting goals and vision, and align them with your values, interests, and passions. You should also adjust and adapt your podcasting strategies and tactics, and optimize them for your needs, resources, and opportunities. You can use goal-setting tools, such as [The SMART Podcast Goals Framework], [The Podcast

Vision Board], or [The Podcast Roadmap], to reevaluate and redefine your podcasting goals and vision. You can also use feedback tools, such as [The Podcast SWOT Analysis], [The Podcast Listener Survey], or [The Podcast Analytics Dashboard], to reevaluate and redefine your podcasting strategies and tactics.

Navigating copyright and legal considerations

Copyright and legal considerations are the rules and regulations that govern the creation, distribution, and use of podcast content and materials. Copyright and legal considerations can affect your podcast's rights, responsibilities, and liabilities, and can also cause disputes, conflicts, or lawsuits. Navigating copyright and legal considerations can help you protect your podcast's intellectual property, reputation, and income, and also increase your podcast's compliance, integrity, and quality.

There are many ways to navigate copyright and legal considerations, depending on your needs, goals, and resources. You can use licenses, permissions, or attributions to navigate copyright and legal considerations. You can also use disclaimers, disclosures, or contracts to navigate copyright and legal considerations.

Some of the best practices for navigating copyright and legal considerations are:

- Understand and respect the rights and obligations of podcast content and materials. You should understand and respect the rights and obligations of podcast content and materials, and avoid infringing, violating, or misusing them. You should also acknowledge and appreciate the original sources, creators, or owners of podcast content and materials, and give them proper credit, recognition, or compensation. You can use licenses, permissions, or attributions, such as [Creative Commons], [Podsafe Music], or [Public Domain], to understand and respect the rights and obligations of podcast content and materials.

- Protect and secure your own podcast content and materials. You should protect and secure your own podcast content and materials, and prevent unauthorized, illegal, or unethical use of them. You should also register and claim your podcast content and materials, and enforce your rights, interests, or benefits over them. You can use disclaimers, disclosures, or contracts, such as [The Podcast Disclaimer], [The Podcast Sponsorship Disclosure], or [The Podcast Guest Agreement], to protect and secure your own podcast content and materials.

- Seek and receive legal advice and assistance. You should seek and receive legal advice and assistance, and consult with a lawyer, an expert, or an authority on podcasting-related legal matters. You should also follow and comply with the laws, regulations, and policies that apply to your podcast, and resolve any legal issues or disputes that may arise. You can use legal resources, such as [The Podcast Lawyer], [The Podcast Legal Guide], or [The Podcast Law Podcast], to seek and receive legal advice and assistance.

CHAPTER 12: FUTURE OF PODCASTING

Podcasting is a rapidly growing and evolving medium, with more than 400 million listeners worldwide and over 2 million podcasts to choose from. Podcasting is also a medium that offers endless possibilities for creativity, innovation, and impact, as podcasters can create and share content on any topic, format, or style. But what does the future of podcasting look like? How can podcasters prepare and adapt to the changes and challenges that lie ahead? In this chapter, we will cover the following topics:

- Predictions and trends for the future of podcasting
- How to stay ahead of the curve

Predictions and trends for the future of podcasting

The future of podcasting is hard to predict, as it depends on many factors, such as listener preferences, technology integration, and industry innovation. However, based on the current state and direction of podcasting, we can make some educated guesses and observations about the possible predictions and trends for the future of podcasting. Some of the most likely and interesting predictions and trends for the future of podcasting are:

- The entire internet will be a podcast. As podcasting becomes more accessible and popular, more and more content and information on the internet will be converted and distributed as podcasts. This means that not only podcasters, but also bloggers, journalists, authors, educators, and other content creators will use podcasting as a way to reach and engage their audiences. Podcasting will also become more integrated with other media, such as video, social media, and live audio, creating a more diverse and immersive podcasting experience.

- Podcasting will become more personalized and interactive. As podcasting becomes more data-driven and AI-powered, podcasting will become more personalized and interactive for both podcasters and listeners. Podcasters will be able to use data and AI to create, edit, and optimize their podcasts, and also to analyze and understand their listeners' behavior, preferences, and feedback. Listeners will be able to use data and AI to discover, consume, and interact with podcasts, and also to customize and control their podcasting experience.

- Podcasting will become more diverse and inclusive. As podcasting becomes more global and local, podcasting will become more diverse and inclusive for both podcasters and listeners. Podcasters will be able to create and share podcasts in different languages, cultures, and perspectives, and also to collaborate and connect with other podcasters across the world. Listeners will be able to access and enjoy podcasts in different languages, cultures, and perspectives, and also to participate and contribute to podcasts in various ways.

- Podcasting will become more profitable and sustainable. As podcasting becomes more mature and mainstream, podcasting will become more profitable and sustainable for both podcasters and partners. Podcasters will be able to monetize their podcasts in different ways, such as ads, sponsorships, subscriptions, products, or services, and also to measure and optimize their podcast revenue and growth. Partners, such as advertisers, sponsors, platforms, or networks, will be able to invest in podcasts in different ways, such as content, exposure, affiliation, or collaboration, and also to evaluate and enhance their podcast return and impact.

How to stay ahead of the curve

The future of podcasting is exciting and promising, but also uncertain and competitive. As podcasting changes and grows, podcasters need to stay ahead of the curve, and keep up with the latest developments and opportunities in the podcasting landscape. How can podcasters do that? Here are some tips and suggestions for podcasters to stay ahead of the curve:

- Stay updated and informed. Podcasters should stay updated and informed about the latest podcasting tools, software, platforms, and directories, and also about the latest podcasting trends, news, and events. Podcasters can use sources and resources, such as The Future of Podcasting: Trends of 2022, What Is the Future of Podcasting in 2023, or Four Podcast Predictions For 2022, to stay updated and informed about the future of podcasting .

- Experiment and innovate. Podcasters should experiment and innovate with their podcasting content, format, and style, and also with their podcasting strategies, tactics, and techniques. Podcasters can use tools and techniques, such as graphic art, creative writing, or code generation, to experiment and innovate with their podcasting content, format, and style. Podcasters can also use tools and techniques, such as email marketing, social media marketing, or podcast cross-promotion, to experiment and innovate with their podcasting strategies, tactics, and techniques.

- Learn and improve. Podcasters should learn and improve their podcasting skills, knowledge, and results, and also learn and improve from their podcasting challenges, mistakes, or successes. Podcasters can use sources and resources, such as [The Podcast Academy], [The Podcast Host Academy], or [The Podcast Movement University], to learn and improve their podcasting skills, knowledge, and results. Podcasters can also use sources and resources, such as [The Podcast Troubleshooting Guide], [The Podcast Burnout Assessment], or [The Podcast Legal Guide], to learn and improve from their podcasting challenges, mistakes, or successes.

- Connect and collaborate. Podcasters should connect and collaborate with other podcasters, listeners, and partners, and create and share value, information, and feedback. Podcasters can use platforms and networks, such as [Podchaser], [Podcorn], or [PodGrid], to connect and collaborate with other podcasters, listeners, and partners. Podcasters can also use forums, chats, or groups, such as [r/podcasting], [Podcasters' Support Group], or [Podcast Movement Community], to connect and collaborate with other podcasters, listeners, and partners.

Conclusion:

You have reached the end of this book, and I hope you have enjoyed and learned from it. In this book, I have shared with you my knowledge, experience, and tips on how to create, launch, and grow a successful podcast. I have also covered some of the common challenges and opportunities that podcasters face, and how to overcome and leverage them.

Here are some of the key takeaways from this book:

- Podcasting is a powerful and rewarding medium that allows you to share your voice, message, and passion with the world.
- Podcasting requires planning, preparation, and execution, and you need to have a clear vision, mission, and goal for your podcast.
- Podcasting involves creating, editing, hosting, and managing your podcast content and materials, and you need to use the best podcasting tools and software for your needs, budget, and goals.
- Podcasting depends on growing and engaging your audience, and you need to use the best podcasting strategies, tactics, and techniques to reach and attract your potential listeners, and to communicate and connect with your existing listeners.
- Podcasting is a dynamic and evolving medium, and you need to adapt to the changes and challenges in the podcasting landscape, and to stay updated and informed on the latest podcasting trends, news, and events.

If you have followed the steps and advice in this book, you should have a solid foundation and framework for your podcast. But remember, this is just the beginning of your podcasting journey. There is always more to learn, improve, and achieve in podcasting. You should always experiment, innovate, and learn from your podcasting challenges, mistakes, or successes.

I want to encourage and motivate you to pursue your podcasting dreams and goals, and to share your podcast with the world. You have a unique and valuable voice, message, and passion, and podcasting is a great way to express and share them. Podcasting can also help you create and share value, information, and impact, and to make a difference in the lives of your listeners and beyond.

You have the potential and the power to create a successful podcast, and I believe in you. I hope this book has helped you in some way, and I would love to hear from you and your podcast. You can contact me at my email address, or follow me on my social media accounts. You can also leave a review or rating for this book on the book's website, or on Amazon. I appreciate your feedback and support.

To conclude this book, I would like to share with you some of the inspiring and successful podcasts that I have listened to, learned from, and loved. These podcasts are examples of how podcasting can be used to create and share amazing content, stories, and messages, and to connect and impact millions of listeners around the world. I hope you will check them out and enjoy them as much as I did.

Here are some of the podcasts that I recommend you listen to:

- **[The Tim Ferriss Show]**: This is one of the most popular and influential podcasts in the world, hosted by Tim Ferriss, the best-selling author of The 4-Hour Workweek and other books. In this podcast, Tim interviews world-class performers from various fields, such as business, sports, arts, and science, and extracts their secrets, habits, and routines that make them successful. This podcast is a goldmine of wisdom, insights, and inspiration for anyone who wants to learn, improve, and achieve more in life.

- **[The School of Greatness]**: This is another inspiring and motivational podcast, hosted by Lewis Howes, a former professional athlete turned entrepreneur, author, and speaker. In this podcast, Lewis interviews some of the most successful and influential people in the world, such as Tony Robbins, Arianna Huffington, and Brené Brown, and shares their stories, lessons, and strategies for achieving greatness in life. This podcast is a source of empowerment, encouragement, and excellence for anyone who wants to pursue their dreams and goals.

· **[The Joe Rogan Experience]:** This is one of the most entertaining and diverse podcasts in the world, hosted by Joe Rogan, a comedian, actor, and UFC commentator. In this podcast, Joe has long and candid conversations with a wide range of guests, such as celebrities, scientists, athletes, and authors, and covers topics such as comedy, culture, politics, and philosophy. This podcast is a mix of humor, curiosity, and intelligence for anyone who wants to have fun and learn something new.

· **[Serial]:** This is one of the most captivating and groundbreaking podcasts in the world, hosted by Sarah Koenig, a journalist and producer. In this podcast, Sarah investigates and narrates a true story over multiple episodes, and explores the details, twists, and mysteries of the case. The first season of this podcast, which focused on the murder of a high school student and the conviction of her ex-boyfriend, became a cultural phenomenon and sparked a global interest in podcasting. This podcast is a masterpiece of storytelling, journalism, and audio production for anyone who loves a good mystery.

· **[TED Radio Hour]:** This is one of the most educational and enlightening podcasts in the world, hosted by Guy Raz, a journalist and podcaster. In this podcast, Guy takes the best talks from TED conferences and expands them into deeper and broader conversations with the speakers and experts. The podcast covers topics such as innovation, creativity, happiness, and leadership, and highlights the ideas and stories that can change the world. This podcast is a fountain of knowledge, inspiration, and wonder for anyone who wants to expand their mind and perspective.

These are just some of the podcasts that I admire and enjoy, but there are many more out there that you can discover and listen to. You can use platforms and directories, such as [Apple Podcasts], [Spotify], or [Google Podcasts], to browse and search for podcasts by category, popularity, or recommendation. You can also use platforms and networks, such as [Podchaser], [Podcorn], or [PodGrid], to rate, review, and follow podcasts and podcasters, and to connect and collaborate with other podcast listeners and creators.

As you listen to these podcasts, I hope you will also think about your own podcast, and how you can use podcasting to express and share your voice, message, and passion with the world. Remember, you have something unique and valuable to offer, and podcasting is a great way to offer it. Don't let fear, doubt, or hesitation stop you from creating and launching your podcast. You have everything you need to start and succeed in podcasting, and I am here to help you along the way.

I hope you have enjoyed this book, and I hope you will enjoy podcasting as much as I do. Thank you for joining me on this journey, and I hope to hear from you and your podcast soon. Until then, keep podcasting, and keep shining!

GLOSSARY:

1. **AAC (Advanced Audio Coding)**: A lossy audio compression format that is used for digital audio broadcasting and streaming.

2. **Ad Insertion**: The process of inserting advertisements into a podcast episode.

3. **Affiliate Marketing**: A type of marketing where a company pays a commission to an affiliate for promoting their products or services.

4. **Analytics**: The collection and analysis of data to gain insights into podcast performance.

5. **Artwork**: The visual representation of a podcast that appears on podcast directories and apps.

6. **Audiogram**: A video clip that features a static image and an audio clip from a podcast episode.

7. **Audio interface**: A device that connects a microphone or other audio equipment to a computer.

8. **Automatic Download**: A feature that allows podcast episodes to be automatically downloaded to a device when they become available.

9. **Back catalog**: A collection of past podcast episodes that are available for download.

10. **Bandwidth**: The amount of data that can be transmitted over an internet connection.

11. **Bed (Podcast Background Music)**: Music that is played in the background of a podcast episode.

12. **Binaural**: A recording technique that uses two microphones to create a 3D stereo sound.

13. **Bit Depth**: The number of bits used to represent each sample in a digital audio file.

14. **Bit Rate**: The number of bits per second that are used to encode a digital audio file.

15. **Bitrate**: The number of bits per second that are used to encode a digital audio file.

16. **Bumper**: A short audio clip that is played at the beginning or end of a podcast episode.

17. **Byte Rate**: The number of bytes per second that are used to encode a digital audio file.

18. **Call-to-action (CTA)**: A prompt that encourages listeners to take a specific action, such as subscribing to a podcast or leaving a review.

19. **Catcher**: A software application that automatically downloads new podcast episodes.

20. **Chapter Marks**: A feature that allows listeners to navigate to specific sections of a podcast episode.

21.   **Clip (as in a short segment)**: A short segment of audio from a podcast episode.

22.   **Clipping**: A type of distortion that occurs when an audio signal exceeds the maximum level that can be recorded or transmitted.

23.   **Compression**: The process of reducing the dynamic range of an audio signal.

24.   **Compressor**: A device or software plugin that reduces the dynamic range of an audio signal.

25.   **Condenser Microphone**: A type of microphone that uses a capacitor to convert sound waves into an electrical signal.

26.   **Content Management System (CMS)**: A software application that is used to manage digital content, such as podcast episodes.

27.   **Cost Per Mille (CPM)**: The cost per thousand downloads or impressions of a podcast episode.

28.   **Cross-Promotion**: The promotion of one podcast on another podcast.

29.   **Cue Point**: A point in a podcast episode where an advertisement or other audio clip can be inserted.

30.   **DAW (Digital Audio Workstation)**: A software application that is used to record, edit, and mix digital audio.

31.   **Dead air**: A period of silence in a podcast episode.

32.   **Decibel (dB)**: A unit of measurement that is used to express the relative loudness of an audio signal.

33.   **Direct Download**: A link that allows listeners to download a podcast episode directly from a website.

34.   **Direct response advertising**: Advertising that encourages listeners to take a specific action, such as visiting a website or making a purchase.

35. **Directory (Podcast Directory)**: A website or app that lists podcasts and allows users to search for and subscribe to them.

36. **Directories**: Plural of directory.

37. **Double-Ender**: A type of remote podcast recording where each participant records their audio locally.

38. **Dynamic Microphone**: A type of microphone that uses a moving coil to convert sound waves into an electrical signal.

39. **Dynamic Range**: The difference between the loudest and softest parts of an audio signal.

40. **Echo**: A type of audio effect that creates a repeating sound.

41. **Embed Player**: A player that is embedded on a website and allows listeners to play a podcast episode without leaving the site.

42. **Encoding**: The process of converting an analog audio signal into a digital format.

43. **Episode Notes**: A written summary of a podcast episode that is included in the show notes.

44. **Equalization (EQ)**: The process of adjusting the balance between different frequencies in an audio signal.

45. **Evergreen Content**: Content that is not time-sensitive and remains relevant for a long period of time.

46. **Peaking**: A type of distortion that occurs when an audio signal exceeds the maximum level that can be recorded or transmitted.

47. **Phantom Power**: A type of electrical power that is used to power condenser microphones.

48. **Plosive**: A type of sound that is produced

when air is expelled from the mouth, such as the sound of the letter "p".

49. **Podcatcher**: A software application that is used to download and manage podcast episodes.

50. **Podcast Directory**: A website or app that lists podcasts and allows users to search for and subscribe to them.

51. **Podcast Network**: A group of podcasts that are produced by the same company or organization.

52. **Podfade**: The phenomenon where a podcast gradually loses listeners and eventually stops producing new episodes.

53. **Podsafe**: Music that can be legally used in a podcast without infringing on copyright laws.

54. **Polar pattern (microphone pickup patterns like cardioid, omnidirectional, etc.)**: The directional sensitivity of a microphone.

55. **Polar Patterns**: The directional sensitivity of a microphone.

56. **Pop Filter**: A device that is used to reduce popping sounds in a podcast episode.

57. **Post-Production**: The process of editing and enhancing a podcast episode after it has been recorded.

58. **Pre-production**: The planning and preparation that goes into creating a podcast episode.

59. **Pre-Roll**: An advertisement that is played at the beginning of a podcast episode.

60. **Promo Code**: A code that is used to offer discounts or other incentives to listeners.

61. **Progressive Uploading**: The process of uploading a podcast episode in segments rather than all at once.

62. **Quality (sound quality)**: The overall sound

characteristics of a podcast episode.

63. **Queue**: A list of podcast episodes that are waiting to be played.

64. **Reflection Filter**: A device that is used to reduce reflections and echoes in a podcast recording.

65. **Remote Podcasting**: The process of recording a podcast episode with participants who are in different locations.

66. **Remote Recording**: The process of recording a podcast episode with participants who are in different locations.

67. **Reverb**: A type of audio effect that simulates the sound of a room or other space.

68. **Room Tone**: The ambient sound of a room or other space.

69. **RSS Feed**: A type of web feed that allows users to subscribe to a podcast and receive new episodes automatically.

70. **Royalty-Free Music**: Music that can be used in a podcast without paying royalties to the composer or publisher.

71. **Samplerate**: The number of samples per second that are used to record a digital audio file.

72. **Scheduling Tools**: Software applications that are used to schedule podcast episodes for release.

73. **SEO (Search Engine Optimization)**: The process of optimizing a podcast's website or other online presence to improve its visibility in search engine results.

74. **Segments**: The individual parts of a podcast episode that are separated by music or other audio cues.

75. **Shownotes**: A written summary of a

podcast episode that includes links and other relevant information.

76. **Sponsors**: Companies or organizations that pay to have their products or services advertised on a podcast.

77. **Sponsorships**: Agreements between a podcast and a sponsor that involve payment for advertising.

78. **Soundboard**: A device or software application that is used to play sound effects and other audio clips during a podcast episode.

79. **Soundproofing**: The process of reducing the amount of sound that enters or leaves a room or other space.

80. **Soundstage**: The perceived location of sounds in a podcast episode.

81. **Stereo**: A type of audio recording that uses two channels to create a sense of space and depth.

82. **Stereographic Sound**: A type of audio recording that uses two channels to create a sense of space and depth.

83. **Stinger (or Sting)**: A short audio clip that is played to indicate a transition between segments of a podcast episode.

84. **Stitching**: The process of combining multiple audio files into a single podcast episode.

85. **Subscribe**: The process of signing up to receive new podcast episodes automatically.

86. **Supercardioid**: A type of microphone polar pattern that is highly directional.

87. **Syndicated content**: Content that is distributed to multiple websites or platforms.

88. **Tagging**: The process of adding metadata to a podcast episode to make it easier to find and organize.

89. **Tailored Ads**: Advertisements that are customized to the interests of individual listeners.

90. **Teaser**: A short audio clip that is used to promote a future podcast episode.

91. **Themes (music)**: Music that is used to create.